HAPPINESS WORKBOOK

A CBT-Based Guide to Fostering Positivity and Embracing Joy

ANNA NAPAWAN, PHD

ROCKRIDGE
PRESS

For general information on our other products and services or to obtain technical support, please contact our Customer Care Department within the United States at (866) 744-2665, or outside the United States at (510) 253-0500.

Rockridge Press publishes its books in a variety of electronic and print formats. Some content that appears in print may not be available in electronic books, and vice versa.

Interior and Cover Designer: Diana Haas
Art Producer: Tom Hood
Editor: Sean Newcott
Production Editor: Matthew Burnett
Production Manager: Jose Olivera

Illustration © Molesko Studio/Shutterstock.
Author photograph courtesy of Ryan Auffenberg.

ISBN: Print 978-1-64876-806-4 | eBook 978-1-64876-232-1
R0

This Workbook
Belongs to:

CONTENTS

"Once we recognize what it is we are feeling, once we recognize we can feel deeply, love deeply, can feel joy, then we will demand that all parts of our lives produce that kind of joy."

—AUDRE LORDE

INTRODUCTION

WELCOME TO THE *HAPPINESS WORKBOOK.* This workbook is designed to help you enjoy more moments of happiness in your daily life. It will support your mental health and well-being by helping you incorporate new ways of thinking, integrate new practices, and appreciate everyday moments so that you will be better equipped to find happiness and embrace joy.

I have always strived to embrace positivity in my life; however, it wasn't until after I became a mother that I began to actively notice and seek out happiness in my everyday life. In raising and spending time with my children, I witnessed them take the world in with awe. Their innate relationship with their environment and their feelings inspired me to embrace a new philosophy, one where I welcomed all of my feelings, coped with moments of discomfort, and warmly invited happiness into my daily life. With this new approach, I experienced more joy through the little things, and my feelings of happiness grew with each new life event.

As a mother, I was particularly struck by how quickly my children were able to move through their wide range of emotions while still managing to be present in the moment. They could be in pain, sadness, or anger and then just as quickly joy, contentment, or calm. Instead of denying their feelings of discomfort, they experienced them and then moved through them, often by shifting their focus to something new or by engaging in activities they enjoyed while continuing to be present. The more I watched my children remain present in their emotions, accept their feelings, and thereby move beyond their feelings, the more I found myself inspired to do the same. I consciously anchored myself each day by embracing small moments; that shift allowed me to take on daily stressors and to focus more on my joyful moments.

In fact, my role as a mother taught me a lot that overlapped with my professional practice as a clinical psychologist. In my practice, I support many individuals who feel that they are struggling to achieve or hold on to happiness. Sometimes my clients are dealing with feelings of low self-worth, anxiety, loneliness, hopelessness, depression, lack of motivation, and negative self-thoughts. Many of my clients want to rid themselves of these feelings, so they resist the sadness and worries and struggle against them instead of feeling them. I encourage my clients to embrace all facets of life while re-centering their focus on daily joys anchored in healthy routines. As a result, they have been able to find happiness even in times of discomfort. I look forward to working with you, throughout the course of this workbook, to find healthy methods of coping with unwanted feelings in order for you to seek out and welcome more happiness into your life.

This workbook is broken down into three parts. **Part One: Understanding Happiness** will explore what happiness is, its foundations, and how to plot your own personal journey toward happiness. **Part Two: Say Yes to Happiness** will walk you through how to achieve happiness through skill and practice. This section delves into how cognitive behavioral therapy (CBT) techniques can help you find new and positive ways of thinking, learn how to lean in to discomfort when it arises, and learn from those experiences. **Part Three: Invest in Your Happiness** focuses on the big picture. It will build on the practical and inspiring CBT exercises from part 2 and teach you how to maintain practices that will help usher in happiness for the long term. Parts 2 and 3 both offer a variety of CBT-based thought-provoking prompts, exercises, and practices that you can use outside the workbook.

This workbook is a productive way to work through negative feelings and stress, but if you experience extreme sadness, depression, debilitating worries, or anxiety, or find that you are struggling to engage in the activities you once enjoyed, I encourage you to seek professional help by a licensed provider. There is no shame—in fact, there is strength—in seeking help or treatment. Whether you choose to use this workbook as an independent guide or in tandem with your current therapy program, follow its headlight on your road to greater happiness.

PART ONE

Understanding Happiness

Let's embark on the first steps of your happiness journey. This part of the workbook explores the definition of happiness—what it is, what it isn't—which will help you begin to understand your personal relationship to happiness. You will explore the benefits of welcoming happiness into your life by striking an even balance with realism and practicality. You will also see how to achieve happiness through cognitive behavioral therapy (CBT) approaches. CBT is a therapeutic intervention through which you examine your cognitions, or thoughts, and associated behaviors in order to consider the various outcomes. CBT was developed by psychiatrist Aaron T. Beck in the 1960s and is still considered the gold standard of psychotherapy treatment because of its evidence-based efficacy in treating depression and anxiety.

ONE

THE POWER OF HAPPINESS

Before you can achieve happiness, you need to define it. I say "you" instead of "we" need to define it because everyone's sense of happiness and journey to achieving it is different. Understanding what happiness means to *you* is the crucial first step. In this chapter, you will unpack degrees of happiness, internal happiness, and external influences on internal happiness. Additionally, you will observe how experiences and feelings can affect or even obstruct happiness so that you can identify any obstacles that may arise along this journey. (You'll explore ways to overcome these obstacles in later chapters.) This chapter will also cover the many ways that fostering happiness can improve your mental health.

WHAT HAPPINESS IS

The concept of happiness may seem simple, and you may feel that you know when you feel happy. To help you be more conscious of the concept, "happiness" might come in different forms, like in the form of confidence or courage. There is a vulnerability that comes with happiness, a sense of openness and a possibility for exploration and learning. Physically, happiness feels warm, or like a sense of calm, fulfillment, and peace in your body. The reason behind this is that on a physiological level, positive emotions are connected to the parasympathetic system of our autonomic nervous system, which regulates our digestive system, heart rate, and breathing rate through the activation of this system. This is why you may notice a slower heart rate and lower blood pressure when feeling happy.

As you experience happiness, you may find that you can let little stressors go and easily navigate the day. You may be able to make decisions more quickly and easily. A sense of happiness can continue to grow and spread to others. You may also find yourself appreciating others more and celebrating their successes, which in turn makes you feel happier and more fulfilled by connecting to people you care about.

Happiness can embody more than just the experience of positive feelings and include the feeling that you have a sense of purpose and that you are honoring your personal values. For some, being a contributing member to society brings fulfillment and happiness. What starts off as a simple feeling grows into experiences, connectivity, values, and engagement with the world, which, with feedback, results in a sustainable cycle of happiness. From here, you can find true happiness.

CONTENTMENT OR BLISS?

Happiness, like all feelings, can be experienced on a spectrum, meaning you can experience degrees of happiness. You can assess the degree of your happiness by using other words for it, like *contentment* or *bliss*. At times you might feel "a little bit of happiness," and for that, you can call it contentment. For example, noticing growth in my garden brings me contentment, as does enjoying a cup of coffee. On the other end of the spectrum, anticipating seeing old friends makes me feel excited, a higher degree of happiness. Think of happiness as a spectrum of feelings that stem from that core feeling. Contentment, on the lower end of the spectrum, relates to feeling satisfied; bliss, on the higher side of the spectrum, means feeling perfect happiness.

Happiness Spectrum

Contentment · Pleasure · Delight · Joy · Excitement · Glee · Bliss

By rating the degree to which you are experiencing a feeling, you will be able to better discern which experiences, activities, or people make you feel happy. Everyone's happiness is derived from different things, and so your happiness is unique to you.

WHAT HAPPINESS ISN'T

It may be enough to discern that emotions like anger, sadness, fear, and disgust are not equal to or related to happiness. Yet it is unwise to dismiss these feelings entirely in your pursuit of happiness because they are natural, normal emotions you experience. Happiness is not the rejection of other more challenging human experiences or emotions. Although it may seem counterintuitive, embracing discomfort can summon happiness in some instances; acceptance of your feelings as you feel them can ultimately help you move with these moments and allow you to refocus on other, happier moments.

Resisting the moments of discomfort makes it harder to access happiness. When you resist discomfort, self-doubt, and low feelings, everyday stress that you were able to handle before becomes overwhelming. Worry can take over, and you may begin to feel symptoms of depression and anxiety.

Think about how children move through their emotions, quickly experiencing negative feelings, letting them go, and moving with ease on to positive feelings. At a young age, people are often allowed, if not expected, to express negative emotions though yelling, crying, sulking, or tantrums. After children express and essentially excise these feelings, they can refocus—sometimes with support and guidance from caregivers—on welcoming, more positive emotions. As an adult, you are socialized not to yell, cry, or throw a fit, but you still need to express these emotions. Some of you have found ways to appropriately let out feelings of anger, hurt, and sadness, while others have been conditioned by upbringings and society to repress feelings rather than express and move through them. As a result, you may cling unhealthily to these feelings and feel stuck or fixated. Or you may express negative feelings in unproductive ways, like using drugs or self-harming, which can result in fixating on negative feelings and then experiencing secondary feelings of guilt or shame for the coping methods you chose and for hurting others and yourself.

No Feeling Is a Wrong Feeling

There is no such thing as a wrong feeling. Feelings may be labeled as negative or positive, but none of the feelings you experience is inherently bad or wrong. It is often out of your control when feelings arise in the first place, either as you work through a thought or as a reaction to an experience. It is important to recognize any and all feelings that you experience, as they can inform how you behave both consciously and unconsciously. Recognizing your feelings is what allows you to make an active choice about how you want to respond and move forward.

A JOURNEY OR A DESTINATION?

We are often fed the idea that once we achieve a form of happiness, we have officially "made it" to our final destination. The truth is that achieving happiness is an ongoing process, a journey. Because you are an ever-developing person whose circumstances change and interests shift, happiness doesn't take on a rigid shape; how you achieve it and how you experience it will change as you change. What once brought joy may one day bring contentment, or what once brought pleasure may one day bring bliss—all of these shifts are normal and indicate that you are evolving and growing.

The steps to achieving happiness may get easier and more enjoyable with time. Other times, seeking happiness may feel like a daunting journey with some bumps along the way. By equipping yourself with the tools to practice enjoying happiness, you will be able to find your footing on the pathway once again.

HAPPINESS AND POSITIVE PSYCHOLOGY

Martin Seligman is a psychologist and writer who popularized the term *positive psychology* in 1996. Positive psychology centers on individual strengths and positive experiences as they influence personal well-being and individual functioning and as a means to achieve happiness. The idea is that you can shift your focus to building upon the positive rather than fixing the negative. Positive psychology, when integrated with CBT interventions, allows you to consider ways to challenge your negative thought patterns and substitute these patterns using techniques that you already have within you.

In other words, the techniques and interventions used in positive psychology highlight the strengths and positive attributes you already possess. As you concentrate on and enhance these skills, you can more readily call upon them to assist you. It can be challenging to become conscious of your skills, so seeking support from a professional can be helpful.

HAPPINESS AND MENTAL HEALTH

Too much or too little of a good thing can affect anyone's mental health. Extreme experiences of happiness can make people feel out of control and manic. An extreme lack of happiness can lead people to feel depressed. When we reach such extreme and uncomfortable states of being, we often seek a better balance of these highs and lows.

Before getting into the right balance of happiness in the remainder of this chapter, consider the well-being of your mind. Mental health comprises everything that you take in; it's a balance of stress and relaxation that stimulates and soothes your mind. You can rest your mind through sleep and meditation. You can exercise your mind by engaging in learning and growing. By doing these things you can experience moments of happiness within a healthy range. Existing solely on either of the two ends of the spectrum of mental health can lead to an imbalance. Finding ways to attain happiness in a balanced way can help support your mental health.

WHY HAPPINESS CAN FEEL ELUSIVE

Happiness can feel elusive because our minds ironically focus on negative emotions in a struggle to move away from these uncomfortable feelings. By focusing on these emotions, our minds *think* they can learn how to combat these negative feelings, and—yes—sometimes this strategy works. More often than not, however, we find ourselves instead fixated on these negative emotions and thus unable to re-center ourselves on other positive or even neutral moments.

Happiness can also feel elusive because you might feel undeserving of it for a whole host of reasons. Perhaps you feel guilt for something you have done in the past, you compare yourself unfavorably to others, or you fail to meet your own measures of perfection. In these instances, you can convince yourself that you are undeserving of happiness. At the same time, deserving or not, you need to recognize that you will not feel happy all of the time. Research suggests that although we have a drive to want to be happy, we are not meant to be happy all of the time. Rather, we need to balance ourselves with the positive and negative emotions, and are meant to feel the other emotions in our lives for the sake of survival.

Further inhibiting your path to happiness is the fact that societal pressures influence your definitions of fulfillment, satisfaction, connectivity, and contributing, which are all factors of happiness. It is important to keep in mind, however, that these facets are subjective; you define them yourself, not through other lenses.

And then there is that societal pressure to present an image of perfection, magnified by social media. Keep in mind that perfection is an unattainable goal, so you need to be realistic. No one is perfectly happy; in fact, it will be your experiences with sadness and adversity that allow you to know what happiness is and to appreciate it. The darker moments highlight the happier ones.

Subjective Well-Being

Subjective well-being is an individual's perception of happiness. Factors like mood, personality, emotions, and life satisfaction contribute to your definition of subjective well-being. It's the general concept that you feel your life is going well. Ed Diener, a psychologist and professor at the University of Utah, developed a three-part model in understanding subjective well-being: experiencing more positive emotions, experiencing fewer negative emotions, and having a positive belief in your life satisfaction. Your well-being is a sense that your life is going in a positive direction based on your own personal perceptions of your experience of well-being.

CONCERNS AND CONDITIONS THAT CAN HINDER HAPPINESS

There are many things that can hinder happiness, such as stress from school or work, relationship stress from friends or family, situational stress like having to make a hard decision, or responsibilities such as caring for others or yourself. Your mindset and temperament can also influence your outlook. Are you typically a glass-half-empty or a glass-half-full type of person? Just knowing this about yourself is helpful. And because your physical body is connected to your mind, your physical health can affect your ability to experience happiness. So not only your temperament and mindset but also your aches and pains can converge and lead to feelings of sadness, stress, and anger. By understanding the concerns and conditions that influence your happiness, you can understand your personal obstacles to happiness and figure out ways to overcome those obstacles in order to achieve it.

SADNESS

Sadness can manifest as personal pain, grief, or loss. Sometimes you may feel hopeless, helpless, disappointed, regretful, or sorrowful. Some people experience more sadness than others. And some people may be subjected to circumstances that elicit more sadness in their lives. Feeling sad is normal and completely acceptable. If your sadness is overtaking much of your day, though, it can hinder your ability to feel happiness.

With all feelings, experiencing a balance is important. Learning how to feel your sadness as a natural reaction to the many stressors in life, and move with it and through it to re-shift focus onto the other facets of your life, is important.

STRESS

Stress can feel like a mental or physical tension. It can live in your body as tension headaches or tension in your neck and back. In modern society, feeling stressed is all too common. You can feel stress from work, home, family, relationships, and more. Like all things, striking a balance is important, as a little bit of stress can be helpful. Stress can help motivate you and drive you to achieve your goals, which can ignite feelings of joy. But you can feel overwhelmed by stress, too, and with too much stress you will not be as able to organize your mind and move forward toward more happiness.

NEGATIVE THOUGHTS

Negative thoughts are cyclical and self-critical. These thoughts repeatedly emphasize negative feelings or narratives about yourself. These thoughts can feel out of our control or automatic in nature. But these thoughts do serve a purpose. Their automatic nature suggests that we evolved to think negatively as a means to self-examine and grow. By carefully examining yourself and evaluating the areas in which you can do better, you can develop into the best version of yourself. As stated with all things, there's a need for . . . balance. It's important to catch negative thoughts and pause them in order to reflect on whether the thoughts are helpful. If the thoughts aren't helpful, then examine what made the thoughts appear and how to shift your internal thinking in order to make the thoughts more useful. Your automatic negative thoughts aren't always well calibrated to support your development, so you need to take the automatic nature out of the process and put a more conscious effort into the thoughts to make them work for you as intended.

SELF-DOUBT

Feeling a lack of confidence is self-doubt. Sometimes your negative thoughts may have taken up real estate in your mind for so long that they have turned into a long-term hit on your self-image. Self-doubt can trick you into thinking, "I'm not good enough" and will impede your ability to seek out happiness, feel successful, and celebrate accomplishments. For some, self-doubt can exist in such a way that pushes you to grow, actively fighting back against the thought that you *can't*, but there is a limit to the ways in which this is helpful. It is important to be vigilant about checking self-doubt when it chips away at your self-love.

ANGER AND ANNOYANCE

Anger is an emotional experience triggered by antagonism toward someone (ourselves included) or something. It can result in increased heart rate and blood pressure. Annoyance, also triggered by an event or person, is irritation. Anger and annoyance can go hand in hand or be felt separately, and they are very similar emotional experiences. Both can pose obstacles to experiencing happiness. Oftentimes, these emotions are secondary to more vulnerable feelings such as stress and sadness, a way of reacting to a deeper pain or hurt. It is okay to feel angry and annoyed, but if these emotions rule your interactions with others, they may be getting in the way of your happiness.

PHYSICAL DISCOMFORT

Because the mind and the body are linked, sometimes you may not be able to enjoy happiness because of physical discomfort. This becomes an unfortunate feedback cycle in which physical discomfort affects your ability to feel happy, leading to even more physical and psychological discomfort. But you can interrupt the cycle. If you track when your body feels discomfort and find it to be consistent, or chronic, it is best to confirm with a medical provider that there is no underlying health condition. In addition, nourishing your body, getting restorative sleep, and attuning to your body's needs will help you embrace more happiness in life.

HAPPINESS IS WITHIN REACH AND CAN CHANGE YOUR LIFE

Even though it feels like lots of things can weigh you down, happiness is within reach. You will learn to acknowledge when sadness, stress, anger, and other negative feelings arise, and find tools to cope with these times as a means to move through them and invite more happiness into your life.

In turn, inviting more happiness into your life can result in being able to handle daily stress and other negative emotions more easily. You will feel your best and behave your best. You will be able to think more efficiently and clearly and will find that you are more productive in all areas of life. You will find that you want to connect more with others, letting them witness your successes and being able to celebrate their successes. You will feel more connected and more able to be vulnerable, furthering connections with the ones you love.

Embracing happiness supports and is supported by you living out your values with a sense of purpose and fulfillment. Again, all of these elements build on one another, which makes happiness grow. And just like this happiness adds to and comes from these global elements, it also adds to and comes from your ability to appreciate the smaller daily moments of joy.

Remember that happiness is a journey, not a destination. Within that journey, it is still important to experience all of the other emotions as well. But by striving for happiness, you can experience the other emotions in a healthier manner, a manner that even allows your positivity to flourish. You will begin to define your own happiness in the following chapters, and you will learn ways to consciously navigate your personal challenges. By plotting out your journey to embrace more positivity, you can begin to learn how to experience happiness in a balanced way.

Discover Your Sources of Happiness

Discovering what makes you happy is very important. This quiz will help you find some of your sources of happiness and illustrate other things that do not bring you happiness, helping you to arrive upon your own definition of personal happiness. Circle the number that goes with the following statements. There is no wrong way to answer.

1 = False   **2** = Slightly False   **3** = Not True or False   **4** = Slightly True   **5** = Very True

1. **I find peace and calm when I'm outdoors.**

   1   2   3   4   5

2. **I enjoy being connected to friends and family.**

   1   2   3   4   5

3. **I have lots of interests and hobbies.**

   1   2   3   4   5

4. **I feel that I have goals and aspirations for my future.**

   1   2   3   4   5

5. **My work or school is fulfilling to me.**

   1   2   3   4   5

6. **Watching movies or shows or reading a book is enjoyable.**

   1   2   3   4   5

7. **I feel energized and motivated after I exercise.**

1   2   3   4   5

8. **I enjoy my solitude.**

1   2   3   4   5

9. **Being with animals brings me contentment.**

1   2   3   4   5

10. **Caring for others brings meaning to my life.**

1   2   3   4   5

11. **Stimulating my mind through learning is fulfilling.**

1   2   3   4   5

Items rated 4 or 5 are sources of happiness. For items rated 3, you are not sure if they bring you happiness; these items merit further exploration. Items rated 1 or 2 may not be sources for your happiness. Your relationship to all these different parts of your life may change; be open to finding joy in new places.

CONCLUSION

Now that you know what happiness is, what happiness isn't, and obstacles that you may encounter on your journey to achieving it, you can continue to develop your own personal definition of happiness. Remember that happiness is a balance: a balance in the emotion itself and a balance with other experiences in life. Experiencing a full range of feelings and moving through moments of discomfort are natural and necessary for everyone. But by knowing that you wish to invite and embrace more happiness in your life and understanding that happiness is a journey, you can look forward to a brighter, more hopeful future. In the next chapter, you will explore the many varied benefits of letting more happiness into your life.

TWO

INVITING A HAPPIER LIFE

In this chapter you will learn the many benefits of inviting more happiness into your life. A happier self can bring better life satisfaction, improve well-being, and foster more personal meaning. Feeling more positive can result in many other mental and physical health benefits, which in turn feed into experiencing more positivity. To be clear, happiness is an emotional state, and although you can experience the feelings of positivity, there is no actual end point at which you attain complete happiness and remain there. Feeling happy is an ongoing journey that requires balance, patience, and hope.

HAPPINESS IS A STATE, NOT A TRAIT

Happiness is a state, not a trait. States are temporal experiences such as thoughts, feelings, and behaviors. States may shift frequently and are susceptible to environmental influences. Traits are enduring patterns of behaviors and can be characterological, meaning the trait is part of your personality. But your state-like experiences influence your trait-like characteristics. As a result of your state of being, you can shift your trait characteristics, as states and traits feed into one another.

For instance, the previous chapter mentioned being a glass-half-full or glass-half-empty kind of person. Having multiple experiences (states) of happiness and interactions with others that are fulfilling can begin to influence your character or personality to become a glass-half-full kind of person. If you've had many negative experiences (states) in life or those times in your life stand out to you in ways that are hard to shake, you may seem like more of a glass-half-empty kind of person.

Let's pause to better understand what it means for someone to have had more negative experiences or more positive experiences that can influence their personality traits. Everyone has had both positive and negative experiences or states that feed into their emotional responses and traits; the more important factor is not how many of each type but rather which type of experiences you choose to focus on. The more you pay attention to the positive moments, no matter the size or the quantity, the more you can build on positivity. By focusing more on the positive moments and finding tools to move through negative moments, you can begin to reside in a more positive emotional state, which will influence your perceptions and, ultimately, your personality traits.

LIFE SATISFACTION, WELL-BEING, AND MEANING

Life satisfaction is how you perceive the various qualities of your life, *perception* being the key. So what factors go into life satisfaction? Future goals, positive self-esteem, and having a generally positive outlook. Having a direction in life, being future-oriented by setting personal life goals, and setting forth on a pathway to obtaining these goals all contribute to life satisfaction.

Moreover, having positive self-esteem, or viewing yourself in a positive way and noting the unique attributes, values, and qualities you like, will improve life satisfaction. On the other hand, feeling more negative about your attributes and having poor self-esteem result in less life satisfaction. Generally, having a positive outlook on life and being hopeful and optimistic can lead to better life satisfaction.

On a related note, well-being is a personal construct that includes elements like positive emotions, engagement, relationship, meaning and purpose, and accomplishment. Meaning is another personal construct that encompasses fulfillment, purpose, self-esteem, and well-being. Often, personal meaning extends beyond yourself and into your community, your contributions to society, and the variety of ways that you can find purpose in the larger context of the world.

These concepts provide an overarching view of happiness. Throughout this workbook, you will focus on the day-to-day elements of positivity to increase your sense of life satisfaction, well-being, and meaning.

THE BENEFITS OF FEELING HAPPIER

There are a number of incredible benefits to experiencing more happiness in your life. Happiness is a feedback loop. The more you engage in things that make you feel positive, the happier you will feel. As you feel happier, you tend to engage in more positive things and continue to see things in a more positive way. This cycle perpetuates happiness. As your positivity grows, you will begin to see health benefits, a better ability to handle stress, improved optimism, increased productivity, and more connectedness with others.

Positive Feelings

**Optimism
(Positive Outlook)**

Prosocial or Positive Behaviors

HEALTH

Researchers have found that feeling happy can lead to a number of physical health benefits. Feeling happier can support a stronger immune system because of a decrease in damaging stress levels; it also can decrease your risk for cardiovascular disease because of lower blood pressure and act as a buffer against the experience of pain. Feeling happy leads to greater self-care, like eating a more balanced diet and participating in more physical activity. It also improves your sleep. In essence, embracing positivity can help you feel less physical distress.

STRESS IS LESS

Feeling happier helps you combat stress. Researchers have found that cortisol, a hormone associated with stress, is produced at a lower level in happier people. In practice, happiness grants you more bandwidth to handle daily life stressors. It enables you to access your coping skills more readily, and it renders those coping skills healthier and more effective, efficient, and adaptive.

PRODUCTIVITY

Feeling happy can lead to increased productivity in the workplace, which can extend to being productive outside work as well. The happier you feel, the more optimistic and motivated you are, resulting in you working harder. You also are able to think more clearly, effectively, and efficiently and make fewer mistakes. As you become happier, you work better with others because you can communicate and collaborate more effectively. Your positivity is contagious, as others are drawn to you, leading to a more productive environment all around. If you feel happier about your life, you will be more invested in everything you do. The more invested you are, the more productive you are. Plus, if what you are doing is fulfilling, it will add to the sense of positivity and, cyclically, your productivity.

CREATIVITY

As you embrace happiness, you gain mental bandwidth to be creative, and being more creative can be exciting, leading to even more happiness. Creativity lets you develop new ideas, allowing you to be more innovative and approach problems in new ways. Similar to how happiness leads to more productivity, happiness allows for more creativity, as you have more ability to think outside the box and approach problems in novel ways. As you're inspired to be more creative, you can explore parts of your identity through unconventional ways such as writing, music, or art. While you are creative, you can find a sense of meaning. The bottom line: being creative just feels good.

SOCIAL CONNECTIONS

One of the benefits of and reasons for happiness is increased social connection. Humans are communal people who need a sense of connection with others as a means for security. When you connect with people, you feel happier; your brain is proof because when you interact socially, your brain releases oxytocin, a feel-good neurotransmitter. As you begin to feel happier around other people, other people will feel happier around you and want to be near you, fostering your relationships, deepening your connections, and furthering your happiness.

SELF-CONFIDENCE

Happiness can bring about feelings of self-confidence. Self-confidence is the opposite of self-doubt. It's feeling assured in yourself, knowing how to make a decision, and trusting your own abilities. Being happy affords you an opportunity to examine your internal drives and motivations more closely because you are handling stress more effectively. Through this examination, you will begin to trust your abilities and judgments, experience more success, and build your self-confidence.

OPTIMISM

Feeling happier can increase your optimism, which in turn lets you become even happier. Optimism means embracing the positivity around you and seeing the world in a more positive light. Highlighting the positive makes other people want to be around you more, which, as you learned earlier, increases happiness. Optimistic people expect to experience more positivity, which helps them really be in the moment when those positive experiences happen.

SELF-COMPASSION

Having more self-compassion will lead to more happiness, and more happiness will lead to self-compassion. People with depression, for instance, tend to be more self-critical or judgmental. Practicing more self-compassion by giving yourself a bit of grace can help address the negative thought patterns and can help you view yourself in a more positive light.

DEFINE HAPPINESS FOR YOURSELF

Perhaps the most important part of experiencing happiness stems from how you perceive your own happiness. It is subjective and dependent on you to define. First, locating various sources of happiness is helpful (see the Discover Your Sources of Happiness quiz on page 14). Do you find joy in connecting with others? Do you find yourself driven and inspired by your work or studies? Do your hobbies and interests bring you fulfillment? Do you enjoy the peace of solitude or connecting with nature?

One way to learn about your personal definition of happiness is to consider an ideal day. Is this a day in which you are accomplishing several tasks? Is this a day you are taking it easy and enjoying the day moment by moment? Or is this a day you are spending with friends and family, sharing an activity together? By envisioning your day, you can begin to suss out the elements that define happiness for you. Your own happiness will need to be defined and then redefined as you continue to develop in your life.

EMBRACE REALISTIC EXPECTATIONS

Having realistic expectations is necessary when taking on a new task, especially a task in which you are engaging in a mental shift to accept more happiness into your life. As mentioned earlier, inviting happiness entails achieving a balance with, not an elimination of, the other emotions. It's evolutionarily necessary—needed for survival, to recognize threatening signals in the world—to feel sadness, pain, disgust, and worry. Thus, it's only realistic to accept that you will continue to experience these other emotions; the hope here is that you will learn many happy-driven ways to more quickly move through the lower feelings to shift to more positive emotions.

"Achieving" happiness is not obtaining perfection, and happiness is not a final destination. It's an ongoing journey, and it takes cognitive effort to preserve an open and positive mindset. As your relationships with people and the world evolve, so, too, will your relationship with happiness. This constant recalibration means that what you once did to achieve happiness may not always work—a signal of growth, not a setback. Your ability to experience happiness will need to grow, too.

SET HAPPINESS GOALS THAT MOTIVATE YOU

Setting up goals in order to experience more happiness in your life can be helpful. These goals need to motivate you rather than act as a barrier to your achievements. Before you settle on what your happiness goals are, consider a few helpful tips. First, your goals need to be attainable and realistic. Setting small goals that you know you can reach and slowly making the goals just a little bit more challenging can help you stretch your skills. What is an attainable happiness goal? Here's one: Take two minutes each day to appreciate a moment outside. The time frame is reasonable, and being outside can mean many things: standing on your stoop, going for a walk, standing by an open window. Setting an attainable goal will motivate you to continue your practices of happiness.

Seeing how you grow in objective, measurable ways can be motivating because you can actually witness your growth. So how do you set a measurable happiness goal? Let's say you find fulfillment in connecting with others. Setting a goal to meet one friend for coffee each week is attainable and measurable. You can slowly increase this measurable goal by expanding your social network and reaching out to more distant friends in an effort to bring more connectivity, which can bring on more happiness.

And don't forget to celebrate achieved goals to help motivate yourself even more. The celebration can be big or small, but it needs to acknowledge your accomplishment in reaching your goal which will help motivate you to continue to strive for your goals.

HOW TO BEGIN THE PURSUIT OF HAPPINESS

One good first step is to focus on the motivating factors for wanting to feel happier. You can use awareness of what motivates you as an anchor to inspire you to feel more positive. Through this awareness you can begin to commit to being happier, which means you are in the mindset and can begin to carve out the pathway to a happier lifestyle. Through this process you should remain flexible, as growth isn't always linear and there may be parts of this process that can be challenging. Having a flexible viewpoint on how to achieve happiness keeps you open to a variety of ways to invite more positivity into your life. As you mentally prepare yourself for the pursuit, it's helpful to set up your environment to begin the process.

Create an environment that helps foster your happiness, since what you see regularly in your home can remind you of your pursuit to include more joy in your life. Your environment includes where you live, operate, learn, and grow. You may not control all the elements of your environment, but you can create a daily routine to begin and end the day. Finding a way to start your day a certain way can set you up for success. This could mean waking up to coffee or tea, or beginning your day listening to a podcast, playlist, or uplifting song. You can ground yourself by reading or saying a mantra, reading a daily blog, or watching uplifting news. It is good to wind down your day with a similar routine.

BE PREPARED FOR CHALLENGES AND OBSTACLES

Challenges will continue to arise throughout this process of embracing more happiness in your life. These might feel like setbacks, but know that they are not. It is only natural to experience a "bump" along the journey toward happiness. These bumps can arise from changes in mood, feelings of self-doubt, or even environmental factors that are beyond your control. Obstacles aren't setbacks. They require you not to restart but rather to pick up where you left off with some extra learning in tow.

A HEALTHY SENSE OF HAPPINESS TAKES TIME

Learning a new skill takes time, and practicing the new skill in order to achieve a new mindset takes even more time. The way you currently engage in and respond to situations is a pattern you have likely practiced for many years. You only recently might have decided to shift the way you think, feel, or behave. Teaching your brain to use new ways to think and to take on a more positive outlook means you have to teach your mind to use neural networks that are less traveled. Your brain will automatically want to go on its familiar route, so you have to work consciously to travel down new neural pathways (that already exist). This takes a lot of time and conscious practice before it can become more automatic. Be patient with yourself as you unlearn old ways and then learn new ways.

CONCLUSION

There are so many wonderful benefits to inviting more happiness into your life, such as improving your physical health, managing stress, growing in creativity and productivity, and improving your relationships. Setting realistic expectations, establishing measurable goals, and preparing for obstacles will enable you to be more receptive to moments of positivity. In the next chapter, you will learn about cognitive behavioral therapy techniques, concrete tools you can use to actively invite more happiness into your life.

THREE

ACHIEVING HAPPINESS THROUGH CBT

In this chapter, you will learn how to invite happiness into your life by exploring the foundational concepts of cognitive behavioral therapy. Cognitive behavioral therapy (CBT) techniques will help you take on the mental blocks that influence how you perceive and experience the world. Your perceptions can be skewed or biased, which can result in you experiencing feelings of sadness, doubt, and isolation. By learning more about your perceptions and biases, you can begin to perceive things in a more balanced way. Doing so will enable you to have balanced experiences, which will make you feel happier.

WHAT IS CBT?

CBT is a form of therapy that involves examining cognitions or perceptions and how these cognitions relate to patterns of behavior. CBT is structured, often short-term treatment that is goal-oriented and focused on addressing specific problems or symptoms. Aaron T. Beck, a psychiatrist who studied at Yale, developed the treatment approach now known as CBT in the 1960s. He developed it to establish a more systematic manner to treat depressive symptoms by examining negative thought patterns. Since then, there have been multiple variations of CBT; all focus on how we think through the process of examining, challenging, and shifting perceptions and belief systems.

In a nutshell, the CBT approach works by identifying, evaluating, and finding new ways to respond to automatic thought patterns. Automatic thought patterns or negative thought patterns are negative ways people automatically think about themselves. Cognitive distortions are specific types of irrational thought patterns (that can also appear automatically), which we will cover more completely later (see Cognitive Distortions, page 31). In CBT, you will identify emotions and examine how the emotions lead to particular automatic thought patterns. From there, you can begin to identify your beliefs and see how your beliefs are informed by your perceptions. These beliefs, called schemas, are the foundation of your understanding of yourself. Schemas develop early in childhood through the perception and feedback of significant others like our caregivers and siblings.

Given that many thought processes are influenced by early life experiences, these thoughts can take a lot of time to unearth, understand, and possibly unlearn so you can learn new balanced ways to perceive the world. In other words, you may have deeply embedded ways of thinking about and perceiving your environment that affect your ability to experience events in a positive way. First, you need to know and understand your biases, and then you can learn new ways to perceive the world that allow you to embrace more positive moments.

A TOOL FOR MENTAL HEALTH AND HAPPINESS

CBT is effective in treating depression, anxiety, post-traumatic stress disorder, eating disorders, personality disorders, anger problems, and general stress. CBT interventions aim to treat specific problems or symptoms. Some examples of CBT approaches include exposure therapy to counter phobias and fears; writing out thought records, an intervention used to identify negative thought patterns; scheduling activities, an intervention that can help enhance social engagement with others; successive approximation, by which we can achieve larger goals by breaking aspirations down into smaller steps; and progressive relaxation, which helps reduce stress. Specific CBT tools are practical, and in the traditional CBT model, they come with homework to practice outside the therapy hour. The in-between session work helps actualize and put into practice the skills learned.

CBT techniques can address concerns to enable you to invite more happiness. The techniques can help you manage stress or combat cognitive distortions, for example. Cognitive distortions are ways in which our minds trick us; they are flawed, biased ways of thinking. Cognitive distortions come about because our brains like to be efficient and come up with shortcuts. These shortcuts sometimes result in us making generalizations, assumptions, and stereotypes, and they develop through our experiences. These shortcuts are not perfect; they are filled with our biases and our self-critical thoughts. And although we can see how critical thoughts are helpful to propel us to grow, we can also note that when they are overly critical, they can stunt growth. Therefore, it's important to unearth and acknowledge your own cognitive distortions.

From an evolutionary perspective, it was beneficial to be self-critical for survival purposes. Yet cognitive distortions persist in our ways of thinking even now, when we typically don't live in life-or-death situations. As a result, being overly negative can impede your ability to embrace the positivity that does exist.

While some CBT techniques help you examine cognitive distortions, other CBT techniques help you recognize faulty beliefs that impede problem solving; still other CBT interventions can help you investigate other automatic negative thoughts.

THE SCIENCE BEHIND CBT TECHNIQUES AND METHODS

CBT techniques and methods are measurable, data-driven interventions, so it is possible to determine the effectiveness of this therapeutic approach. This approach is so measurable because interventions often focus on a specific action, allowing change to be tracked. For example, a thought record allows you to track your negative thought patterns. As you continue keeping the record, you will clearly see any progress in your ability to identify and decrease the thought patterns.

Furthermore, CBT examines problems through five domains: situations, thoughts, emotions, physical feelings, and behaviors. These areas are intertwined, but you can begin to see which domains are being affected in a given experience and how they may influence your core beliefs or negative thoughts. By breaking problems down into these domains, CBT makes them more approachable, tangible, understandable, and easily targeted.

PRACTICAL STRATEGIES TO BUILD A TOOLBOX FOR EVERY DAY

CBT offers very practical strategies and tools such as journaling, thought recording, activity scheduling, deep breathing, muscle relaxation, and use of imagery. As you progress through this workbook, you will learn many different coping strategies, or "tools." Having a large repertoire of so-called tools for your toolbox is helpful so you have many different coping skills to address the various stressors, situations, and feelings that arise. With continued practice in knowing the exact tool to use, not only will you be more readily able to identify the tool you need, but the tool may be more effective and efficient. With a toolbox full of a variety of tools, such as deep breathing, taking a walk, or saying a personal mantra, you will be able to handle larger problems in your life. As you build up your personal toolbox and learn to use your tools, you will refine your ability to know the exact tool to combat the types of cognitive distortions discussed in the next section.

COGNITIVE DISTORTIONS

As mentioned earlier, cognitive distortions are ways in which your mind tricks you—flawed, biased ways of thinking. CBT techniques can take on cognitive distortions like the ones listed here to help you progress on your journey toward happiness.

Balancing All-or-Nothing Thinking

All-or-nothing thinking is a type of cognitive distortion, or error in thinking, in which perceptions are skewed to one extreme or another; it can be challenging to perceive in the middle or gray zone. When you engage in all-or-nothing thinking, you may find yourself saying or feeling in absolute ways, such as "That will *never* happen for me" or "Nothing *ever* goes my way." By first catching this kind of thinking through recognizing the use of words such as *always*, *never*, *ever*, and *nothing*, you can begin identifying this cognitive distortion. The recognition is the hardest step, and then from there you can begin to find ways to see the shades of gray as you solve problems.

Managing Automatic Negative Thoughts

Automatic negative thoughts are typically negative self-appraisals. Automatic negative thoughts often lead to feelings of low self-esteem, guilt, and shame. These thoughts can feel overwhelming to change because they are, by nature, automatic, and they often stem from core beliefs that developed early in life. By first recognizing the thoughts and then developing new habits, you can slowly make progress in challenging them. Some common negative thoughts are *I'm stupid*, *I don't deserve anything*, *I'm not good enough*, *I can't do this*, and *I'm really bad at that*. *I should just give up*.

If you examine when these thoughts first appeared, you may notice that there may have been moments in your upbringing that resulted in you feeling this way. Since these thoughts have been with you for a while, it will take time to shift the thinking. Challenging the thoughts and replacing them with more measured and compassionate ways of thinking can sound like *This situation or problem is hard*; *I will work hard and do my best*; *This is challenging, but I have some experience and skill*; and *I will try my best*.

These kinds of replacements shift the negative thinking while recognizing that the situation may still be challenging.

Inviting Rather Than Rejecting the Positive

Don't force positive thoughts; rather, invite them in. Inviting positivity can be really challenging. You may experience moments of positivity and immediately reject them because you don't feel you deserve positivity. Your automatic negative thoughts may kick in. You may believe that accepting the positive moment may jinx other possibilities.

Here's how you can invite positivity in. First, you need to interrupt your cognitive distortions. Second, you need to be realistic. You will continue to have challenging moments and days when embracing positivity is difficult. By recognizing and accepting that you will still experience challenges, you are opening yourself up to all of the other opportunities to invite positivity into your life. Rather than rejecting or expecting the positivity, you'll acknowledge and appreciate it.

Avoiding Minimizing or Magnifying

Minimizing and magnifying are other types of cognitive distortion that can affect the way you view yourself. You may find yourself minimizing positive events, such as achievements and accomplishments, while magnifying the times you have made errors and mistakes. This imbalance can feed into your self-esteem and how you view your own abilities. It can ultimately have bearing on your perception of your own happiness.

You can examine this by noting your successes, being present in them, and even celebrating them, no matter how small. You can begin to challenge the times you overemphasize your mistakes, examining how the error may not necessarily come from within but rather result from a combination of causes, such as external and circumstantial events that anyone would find challenging. By taking a more balanced approach, you may find yourself being more forgiving to yourself and less critical, which will lead you to feel better about yourself and happier.

"Should" Statements

"Should" statements are stated expectations of yourself that likely won't be met. They include statements like *I should have done this* and *Why didn't I think of that?* They are not motivating; in fact, they lead to shame, discourage productivity, and increase anxiety. While they may sound like they encourage you to act, there is an implied adjunct to the "should" statement, as in *I should have exercised yesterday, but I didn't.* The "should" statement actually reflects an unstated but very present sense of failure. However, we can acknowledge "should" statements and turn them into wonder, such as *I wonder what I need to do to get this done* or *I'm curious how I can approach this problem differently next time.* Through this shift we can open ourselves up to possibilities rather than stunting our abilities.

Letting Go Instead of Taking It Personally

We often can take negative events or words personally. We think during difficult times that we are at fault. Doing this makes sense because if we take the blame, maybe we can take control and do something about the situation. Our minds want to develop, grow, and be better, and one of the ways they do this is by personalizing events.

But it is important to stop and examine these moments. When you begin to take something personally, can you really control the situation? Can you really grow from it and change things? You may find that only a small portion of the time this is the case. It could be that there is no growth opportunity, but rather it poses an impediment to you seeing yourself in a positive way. When you find yourself taking something personally, take a pause, evaluate, and consider the external factors that may be playing a larger role in the situation.

Catastrophizing

When we believe the worst-case scenario will happen, we are engaging in what's called *catastrophizing*. We may do this for a number of reasons: as a means of preparation, as a way to predict the future, or because of a belief that if we anticipate the worst possible scenario, it won't actually occur. If we prescribe a certain outcome without allowing the situation to unfold organically, we'll feel worried and anxious as a result.

If you recognize you're playing a scenario out in your mind or even with others, it limits your ability to be open to how things may actually unfold. Similar to any thought distortion, in order to shift it, we have to recognize that we are doing it. By taking a moment to pause in this process, we can allow ourselves to be open to other possibilities and prevent ourselves from engaging in negative energy by anticipating the worst.

Redirecting the Focus Given to Negative Thoughts

Negative thoughts will continue to appear, but there may be times to engage with them, examine them, and develop a new relationship with them. Yes, sometimes no matter how much you challenge the thought, you will be unable to shift your core belief about yourself. But sometimes you will be able to redirect your attention to new, more positive thoughts in an effort to move on. The process of refocusing on more positive thoughts is a helpful strategy at times in order to move forward. As negative thoughts continue to appear, notice them, spend a moment with them, and then redirect your focus onto more inspiring thoughts. This process can help motivate you to engage in joyful moments.

How to Make Room for Happiness

As you make room for happiness, you will embrace change. Change can be challenging and frustrating but can offer tremendous growth. There are stages in life during which you may not be ready to embrace change. You can determine exactly where you are in the process of embracing change by using the transtheoretical model of change. The following questionnaire will help determine where you are in accepting change in order to achieve more happiness in your life.

Circle the phrase that best fits your state of mind as you prepare to change to make room for happiness:

1. I don't know what I'm doing or feeling.

2. I'm not really sure how to invite happiness into my life.

3. I really want to feel happier; I just don't know how to do it yet.

4. I'm working hard to embrace a new mindset, and it's challenging at times.

5. I have embraced a new way of thinking and feeling but need to make sure I maintain it.

6. I've experienced a setback but would like to try to solidify some skills.

Using the number of the phrase that you circled in the preceding list, look to the following key to see where you are in terms of readiness for change. The fact that you grabbed this workbook indicates that part of you is motivated to feel differently. Most likely you will be in stage 3, 4, 5, or 6. Keep in mind that you may shift your stage-of-change, so you can revisit the question anytime.

1. **Precontemplative:** You're not really sure how or what you want to change, but part of you wants a difference. If this is where you are, consider what parts of your life you would like to be different.

2. **Contemplative:** You're not sure if you want to change, but you are considering that things need to be different in your life. You may have a better grasp as to what you want different in your life, and you are starting to identify those parts of your life.

3. **Determination:** You know you want something different in your life, and you are finding the steps to get there even if you don't feel sure all the time. By grabbing this workbook, you are plotting your path to shift the direction of your life and are developing a plan of what you want different in your life.

4. **Action:** You are goal oriented and ready to achieve. You find moments of challenge that feel like setbacks at times. You know how you want to change, and you have set your goals in order to change. This could be your first time visiting this particular workbook, or you may be returning to this workbook.

5. **Maintenance:** You have embraced change in a new mindset and are stable in understanding it and maintaining it. You have achieved a balance in your life, but you are seeking more coping skills or strategies to maintain the positivity in your life.

6. **Relapse:** You have found tools and at times felt stable but experienced a setback in the process. Although the term *relapse* may have a negative connotation, it's not necessarily the case. In this particular instance, relapse may mean that you have felt more emotionally balanced at one point in time through your personal efforts. You would like to return to feeling more balanced once again.

Although these stages feel like steps, they are not necessarily linear. You may find yourself jumping around in where you feel ready to engage in change. For instance, you might find yourself in the contemplating stage-of-change, and as you learn more, you feel less clear about change and shift to the precontemplation stage-of-change. Also, people commonly move from maintenance to relapse. That is fine, and when you feel ready to make change, you can always revisit the CBT skills that you learn in this workbook.

CBT SKILLS LAST A LIFETIME

CBT skills are realistic and approachable and can be revisited throughout your lifetime. The interventions can be adjusted and tailored specifically to you. For instance, identifying, expressing, and coping with your emotions are key components of CBT, and yet these are skills we continually work on, no matter the age. Younger people may work on labeling their feelings and finding an adaptive way to express them through verbalization, like stating, "I'm mad," for instance. In adulthood, we work on the same things but in more sophisticated manners to explore emotional states, clearly verbalize these states, and find healthy ways to cope. CBT interventions apply across a lifetime in order to improve moods, address behaviors, enhance connections, and bring more positivity. As you continually develop, you may need to revisit and possibly adapt the CBT skills to your current goals and experiences.

READY, SET, GO!

Now that you have a foundational grasp on your definition of happiness and you are thinking about your readiness to change and your potential obstacles on the journey, you can begin to work on the skills that will invite more happiness into your life. Be kind to yourself and know that there is no perfect way to begin this journey. There will be times when things are challenging, and those are not necessarily setbacks but normative stressors everyone experiences. The ways in which you navigate those times can be a measure of how you have embraced some of the tools you have learned.

In part 2: Say Yes to Happiness and part 3: Invest in your Happiness, you will be invited to engage in concrete CBT interventions to help you embrace more positivity by examining your thought processes, your environment and the ways you engage with it, your social connectivity, and your mind-body connection. You will be invited to explore your internal self and find ways to integrate the skills into your life in order to embrace overall happiness and little moments of joy.

CONCLUSION

This chapter demonstrated how CBT techniques can help you achieve a more positive perspective of your experiences through the examination of your perceptions and thoughts. It helped you gain a better grasp of your personal readiness to engage in change. In the next chapter, you will continue to build on these skills to pause and acknowledge former, less balanced ways of thinking. Additionally, in the following chapters you will begin to develop new skills to see the world more positively and think more joyfully, which will translate to happier ways of engaging with your environment through your behaviors.

PART TWO

Say Yes to Happiness

In the second part of this workbook, you will continue to build on your personal definition of happiness, add to your foundational CBT understanding, and integrate practical exercises to invite more happiness. In this part, the chapters are broken down into engaging prompts to inspire reflection, exercises to write and engage your thoughts, affirmations, quotations, and practices to do outside the book and integrate into your life to help you embrace a more balanced experience. The practical exercises in the workbook may inspire you in the immediate moment, and you can continue to revisit and explore these exercises daily or weekly to help you engage in rituals that enhance happiness in your life.

FOUR
PRACTICE POSITIVITY

In this chapter you will begin to practice positivity and discover tools to help you better navigate the negative moments in life. You will learn how to identify stressors and negative thought patterns as well as sources of happiness. You will explore routines to embrace happiness and focus on everyday moments in order to invite more joy into your life. As you progress through this chapter, remember that there is no correct way to answer the prompts. Some of these prompts, exercises, and practices may be challenging at times, but that's okay because you will have your own unique journey toward happiness.

THE OXFORD HAPPINESS QUESTIONNAIRE

The Oxford Happiness Questionnaire was developed by psychologists Michael Argyle and Peter Hills at Oxford University to determine your personal relationship to happiness. Following are a number of statements about happiness. Please indicate how much you agree or disagree with each, according to the following scale:

1 = Strongly Disagree **2** = Moderately Disagree **3** = Slightly Disagree
4 = Slightly Agree **5** = Moderately Agree **6** = Strongly Agree

Remember that there are no "right" or "wrong" answers (and no trick questions).

1. I don't feel particularly pleased with the way I am. (R)

    1   2   3   4   5   6

2. I am intensely interested in other people.

    1   2   3   4   5   6

3. I feel that life is very rewarding.

    1   2   3   4   5   6

4. I have very warm feelings toward almost everyone.

    1   2   3   4   5   6

5. I rarely wake up feeling rested. (R)

    1   2   3   4   5   6

6. I am not particularly optimistic about the future. (R)

    1   2   3   4   5   6

7. I find most things amusing.

    1   2   3   4   5   6

8. I am always committed and involved.

1   2   3   4   5   6

9. Life is good.

1   2   3   4   5   6

10. I do not think that the world is a good place. (R)

1   2   3   4   5   6

11. I laugh a lot.

1   2   3   4   5   6

12. I am well satisfied about everything in my life.

1   2   3   4   5   6

13. I don't think I look attractive. (R)

1   2   3   4   5   6

14. There is a gap between what I would like to do and what I have done. (R)

1   2   3   4   5   6

15. I am very happy.

1   2   3   4   5   6

16. I find beauty in some things.

1   2   3   4   5   6

17. I always have a cheerful effect on others.

1   2   3   4   5   6

18. I can fit in (find time for) everything I want to.

1   2   3   4   5   6

19. I feel that I am not especially in control of my life. (R)

    1   2   3   4   5   6

20. I feel able to take anything on.

    1   2   3   4   5   6

21. I feel fully mentally alert.

    1   2   3   4   5   6

22. I often experience joy and elation.

    1   2   3   4   5   6

23. I don't find it easy to make decisions. (R)

    1   2   3   4   5   6

24. I don't have a particular sense of meaning and purpose in my life. (R)

    1   2   3   4   5   6

25. I feel I have a great deal of energy.

    1   2   3   4   5   6

26. I usually have a good influence on events.

    1   2   3   4   5   6

27. I don't have fun with other people. (R)

    1   2   3   4   5   6

28. I don't feel particularly healthy. (R)

    1   2   3   4   5   6

29. I don't have particularly happy memories of the past. (R)

    1   2   3   4   5   6

Scoring

Step 1. Calculate your score. Items marked (R) should be scored in reverse: for example, if you gave yourself a "1," cross it out and change it to a "6."

Change "1" to "6."

Change "2" to "5."

Change "3" to "4."

Change "4" to "3."

Change "5" to "2."

Change "6" to "1."

Step 2. Add the numbers for all 29 questions. (Use the converted numbers for the 12 items that are reverse scored.)

Step 3. Divide by 29. Your happiness score = the total (from step 2) divided by 29. Interpreting the score:

1: Not happy 2: Somewhat unhappy 3: Not particularly happy or unhappy 4: Mostly happy 5: Very happy 6: Overly happy

What Do These Scores Mean in Using This Workbook?

Balanced Scores

Obtaining a score of 4 or 5 suggests that you are in a balanced range and thus the skills you learn in the workbook will help manage stressful and uncomfortable times.

Obtaining a 3, although in the balanced range, suggests that you may be a little more pessimistic. Thus, it will be helpful to begin to integrate the prompts and practices into your life in order to feel happier.

Imbalanced Scores

A score in the 1 to 2 range suggests that you are probably seeing yourself in a worse situation than reality. In addition to integrating strategies from this workbook into your life, you may find it helpful to seek professional help to support you in examining ways to move through the negative events in your life and to give you some tools to manage stress.

A score of 6 suggests that you are too happy, which can lead to a less successful life. Someone in a constant euphoric state is not equipped to address adversities and may not be motivated to reach goals. Finding strategies to ground you in the moment will be helpful. Should you feel that you have trouble tending to essential areas of your life, seeking professional help can be very useful and healing.

What Stresses You Out?

It's helpful to understand your stress in order to cope with it. Recognizing your sources of stress will allow you to practice ways to engage in more positivity. Write down three major sources of stress for you; these can be more immediate stressors, like paying bills, or general stressors, like navigating a challenging relationship or hopes for a promotion:

1. _____

2. _____

3. _____

Daily Dose of Happiness

Write down a moment that brought you happiness recently.

_____

_____

Building on Breathing

Coping skills are necessary to deal with stressful or unpredictable times. Breathing is an important coping skill, and you have access to it no matter where you are or what you are doing. It's important to breathe in a healthy, calming way. Engaging in regulated breathing can quickly help you manage overwhelming feelings and can be a great addition to your daily routine.

1. Inhale slowly through your nose, focusing on any tension in your body, such as in your shoulders, neck, or belly.

2. Exhale very slowly out through your mouth, elongating your breath as if you are exhaling through a straw and releasing the tension in your body.

3. Inhale again, noticing any thoughts in your mind and focusing on those thoughts.

4. Exhale once again in the same manner and imagine that you are releasing those thoughts out of your mind and body, as if the thoughts are little puffs of air.

5. Repeat this process, taking five to eight breaths in and out.

> As I face the challenges and stressors in my life, I learn new tools to handle and cope with these moments.

Cognitive Distortions

Chapter 3 discussed various types of cognitive distortions, such as all-or-nothing thinking, minimizing the positives, maximizing the negatives, catastrophizing, "should" statements, and taking things personally. It's helpful to identify the flawed ways you may think in order to begin shifting these thought processes. Circle the thought patterns you engage in and try to think of an example of when you engaged in it.

All-or-nothing thinking	Taking the situation personally
Self-blaming	"Should" statements
Magnifying negative events	Minimizing positive events

What You're Grateful For

Reflect on three sources of gratitude.

1. _____

2. _____

3. _____

> "Even a happy life cannot be without a measure of darkness, and the word *happy* would lose its meaning if it were not balanced by sadness. It is far better to take things as they come along, with patience and equanimity."
>
> —CARL JUNG

Grounding to Deal with Stress

Grounding yourself in the everyday—sights, sounds, smells, and feelings—is a helpful way to deal with negative thoughts and negative moments. Noticing your senses is helpful: Can you notice the colors you see in your environment? Can you hear the various sounds inside your body, in your room, and outside the space? Can you notice what you feel, like your clothing, or the support of your seat? Can you smell or taste anything? Take a moment to reflect, and then really focus on one sense. It's easier and more comforting than you may think to be present in a sense that you don't often notice.

Coping Tools

Knowing how to cope with the negative times is always helpful. Circle the coping skills you have used in the past or can see yourself using in the future.

Breathing	Singing	Exercise	Walking	Taking a sip of water
Engaging with nature	Caring for a pet	Gardening	Watching sports	Reading
Cooking	Connecting with others	Journaling	Creating art	Building or repairing things
Cleaning	Meditation	Listening to or playing music	Taking a shower or bath	Other: _____

Active and Passive Coping Tools

In this workbook, you will explore various strategies to help you cope, including both active and passive coping tools. Active coping strategies are those in which you actually shift the way you think or behave in order to cope. For example, active coping skills include using mindfulness and reframing a situation. Passive coping strategies may help you avoid a situation. Some examples of passive coping skills include the use of time, distractions, or an un-orchestrated change in circumstances. Although both types of coping are helpful, it is important to be aware of the coping skill you are using. In your journey to find more happiness, you will practice various active and passive tools, and through practice you will learn which coping tools are easiest for you to use in various circumstances.

Daily Positivity

Daily positivity is important to embrace and can help you refocus the negative moments that occur in life. Positive moments can be found in the little things. Write down three positive little moments that you experienced recently.

1. _____

2. _____

3. _____

MANAGING OUR OVERFLOWING STRESS

Stress can fill our bodies, much the same way that water can fill a cup. It can drip in slowly yet accumulate. It might feel like a steady fill or a sudden flood. All of a sudden you might find your cup spilling over. You can do things throughout the day to slowly empty your cup so you are not overwhelmed by life's stressors. Using this analogy, consider the stressors that can fill your cup and ways you can actively cope and make room for happiness amid normal stress.

Joy in the Everyday

Finding joy in little everyday things is necessary. Consider these moments to be like your daily vitamins. They help you manage your stressors and can help keep your cup from overflowing. Consider your everyday routine and note the times the routine brings you a touch of joy.

_____

_____

Jump-start Your Day

What are three things in your regular routine that help you start off your day?

1. _____

2. _____

3. _____

Body and Mind

As you know, your body and mind are interconnected, and you can easily carry stress in your physical body, leading to soreness and aches. Circle the ways you can address some of the tension in your body.

| Massage | Yoga | Stretching | Heat therapy | Meditation |

| Progressive muscle relaxation | Warm showers or baths | Drinking tea | Slow breathing | Walking |

Magnifying Positivity

Spending time on a positive moment is an important building block to feeling more happiness in general. It can help you notice your strengths and celebrate your successes. Think of a positive moment that happened recently in your life and consider all the details of the event. What happened? What thoughts came up? What exact feelings did you notice? Write down as many details as possible to help magnify the positivity of the experience.

_____

_____

_____

End-of-Day Wind-Down

What are three things in your regular routine that help you wind down your day?

1. _____

2. _____

3. _____

Self-Compassion

Being compassionate to yourself is important as you embrace the discomfort and hardships of life. It's important to take a pause when you notice these moments and say something kind to yourself, such as "It's normal to feel down, and this time will pass." What self-compassionate statement can you say to yourself when a difficult moment arises?

_____

_____

Positive Attributes

When building on positivity, it's important to think about the personal characteristics that you enjoy and feel proud of. Take some time and reflect on what you consider to be your favorite parts of yourself. These can be personality attributes, interests, and things you do. Name as many qualities as possible.

_____

_____

The Power of Journaling

Using your words and finding safe and comfortable ways to tell your personal stories can help you understand and process your experiences, whether they are positive or negative in nature. When you experience chronic stress or trauma, you can feel overwhelmed by your emotions. One way you can organize or process your feelings is through narrating them. Narrating feelings is often what people do in talk therapy, but the simple act of journaling about your experiences can also structure your feelings and help you understand your experiences. Whether through journaling using prompts or freewriting, reflecting in writing about your experiences can help you regulate overwhelming emotions, support your mental health, and assist you in achieving happiness.

Daily Motivation

Getting the day started can be difficult, but noting the things that excite you can often help. Write down a few things that motivate and inspire you.

1. _____

2. _____

3. _____

COGNITIVE TRANSFORMATION

Cognitive distortions are normal. As you recall, cognitive distortions are negatively biased perceptions that include catastrophizing and taking things personally. Everyone engages in them because they are shortcuts in thinking. Once you've identified some of your cognitive distortions, consider transforming your negative thoughts into alternative ways of thinking. Fill in the following chart.

I'm not smart enough. → This task is hard, and I will try my best.

I'm so unmotivated. → I have a lot to do, and I will begin to organize my day.

No one likes me. → I'm working on myself so I can develop
meaningful relationships.

Biased Thinking	→	Cognitive Transformation

CONCLUSION

In this chapter, you examined your degree of happiness in order to know how to integrate some CBT coping tools. En route to greater happiness, you worked to identify some common stressors in your life and some biased thought patterns that can make stressful times more challenging. And you began a healthy shift from this way of thinking to reconnect with personal attributes that are positive and strong. You also explored grounding techniques to better cope with normal stressors. As you move into the next chapter, you will continue to build on these CBT tools to find ways to focus on the good and find greater happiness.

FIVE

FOCUS ON THE GOOD

As you embrace more positive moments in your life, it's helpful to emphasize the good, happy moments, qualities that you pride yourself on, and supportive or comforting environments you inhabit. You can do this by continuing to magnify the positivity you experience, surrounding yourself with uplifting people, and engaging in positive acts. In this chapter, you will continue to build on these skills to shift and challenge your automatic negative thought patterns or cognitive distortions and continue your journey toward happiness. You'll learn more tools that can be added to your toolbox in order to anchor yourself in your successes and accomplishments and enjoy the good in your life.

Setting Goals

List three things you plan to accomplish today. These can be small goals like completing a basic chore or bigger goals like completing a renovation project. Make sure that once you complete a task today, you cross it off your list. This simple list of goals can help you stay grounded in your daily life, and even something as simple as a check mark is a great way to celebrate everyday accomplishments.

1. _____

2. _____

3. _____

Slow Down to See the Good

If you feel pressure to move quickly from one task or feeling to the next, you can miss out on noticing and appreciating the positive. Staying present in the moment and even those in-between moments allows you to take in your surroundings, as if you are a child, amazed by the world around you. This can be a hard practice to take on, given busy lives, but aim to take a moment to reflect on where you are, what you are doing, and how you feel every day. This could be a moment where you absorb the amazement of the time and patience it took for the trees around you to grow or how a large-scale building was constructed from bottom to top in great detail. It could be noticing the complexity and beauty in an everyday item that you use to get through your day, such as your house keys or the faucet in your kitchen sink. When you give yourself a moment to take in and appreciate the world around you, you'll begin to see all the good that surrounds you and adds to your day. Reflect on two recent moments in which you were able to slow down and see the good in the moment.

1. _____

2. _____

Let the Past Go!

Oftentimes when you feel fixated on past events, you might find yourself saying, "I should have …" Substituting a more productive and hopeful word like *tried* for the word *should* can help you move on from your past and embrace the happy possibilities of your future. For example, try thinking about a past event that might make you feel sad or regretful and telling yourself, "Given what I knew then, I made the best decision at that time." In the space that follows, consider some key "should have" moments from your past and rewrite those thoughts with grace, understanding, and forgiveness.

I should have worked harder. ➔ **I tried my best given the circumstances.**

_____

_____

_____

> I am embracing change, trying new things, and shifting my routines. Despite the fact that these things are hard to do, I am trying, and I am strong in challenging myself to grow.

Daily Dose of Smile

Noticing the positive in your everyday life is important and quite similar to giving yourself a daily vitamin boost. Write down three things that made you smile today. Take a moment to reflect on the simple things that often make you smile, such as enjoying a sunset or appreciating the growth of a plant.

1. _____

2. _____

3. _____

How to Get a Daily Dose of Happiness

We know that focusing on the good can improve our moods and help us feel more positivity, which will then continue to grow. Yet getting a daily dose of happiness, similar to a daily dose of a vitamin, can be challenging. One unexpected way to infuse yourself with this daily dose is to reframe your thinking. Take a time that isn't necessarily considered to be a time of positivity and turn it into one. For example, your commute time to work can be *your* time to listen to that podcast you enjoy. By consciously recognizing your daily dose of happiness each day, you can continue to build on feelings of positivity.

Decorate Your Space to Feel Good!

Decorating your space, at home or at work, can give you a refreshed, cleansed, and positive feeling. This could mean painting a room, rearranging your furniture, changing a light fixture, or decorating your walls with new artwork. Also, by cleaning up spaces in your house, you can clear your mind and organize yourself through your environment. Whether it be redecorating or organizing, consider how a simple shift in your everyday environment can shift your mood. How can you switch up your space a little?

Positive Mantra

Positive sayings are helpful to inspire us, ground us, and prevent us from dwelling on negative experiences. Some positive mantras are "I've got what it takes to do this!" "I'm patient and learning and growing!" and "I recognize the change I want, and I'm doing my best to make a shift." Take these inspiring words and make them your own. Feel free to pull from what feels overwhelming and challenging right now and make the mantra specific to that. What is a mantra you can say to inspire yourself?

Have a Laugh!

Laughter is a wonderful tool in moments of stress—we feel supported when we laugh with others, joyful when we can laugh at something humorous, and uplifted out of a low state. Turning to humor in darker moments can help you move through feelings of pain or discomfort and help you shake those feelings off rather than lingering in them, creating a healthy balance of sadness and happiness. Think about how you usually encounter humor, such as talking to a funny friend or watching a comedy. List some of your favorite ways to access and enjoy a laugh.

1. _____

2. _____

3. _____

Fill Yourself with Goodness

There is so much to be consumed in the news, social media, and other forms of entertainment; sometimes it can feel overwhelming, but there is still so much goodness all around us. Think about different ways you can access and engage with media of all kinds to intentionally take in stories, images, videos, and experiences that focus on acts of kindness. Circle the ways that you can invite more encouraging and happy news into your life and do them.

- **Watch videos of strangers engaging in acts of kindness.**

- **Listen to podcasts with a message of positivity.**

- **Take part in Good Samaritan work through volunteering or fundraising.**

- **Help a community member, neighbor, or friend.**

- **Pay it forward by donating to a charity or cause important to you.**

Check Your Surroundings

Go to at least one place this week that brings you positivity and happiness, such as a park, art gallery, or animal shelter. By interacting with places that bring you positivity or peace, you can embrace more joy into your life. Use this space to list the various places that make you feel positive.

_____

_____

_____

_____

Connecting with Nature

Research has shown that connecting with nature and exposing yourself to a green environment can help offset mental health disorders like anxiety and depression. Embracing the world outside can feel daunting for some because it means leaving your home and being out in a public setting. Setting realistic goals by setting aside a small amount of time or not going too far from your home can help you spend more time outdoors. Little by little, you may be able to increase your time outside or how far you travel. You can even embrace the outdoors by enjoying your coffee or tea by a window and taking a quiet moment to observe what you see. You could also spend some time on your patio, porch, balcony, deck, or front steps to listen to the sounds of birds, the rustle of the trees, or the chatter of your neighbors. Wherever and however you can connect with nature, take note of all of the green space around you or how the leaves are turning or the blossoming of new flowers. Another way to connect with nature is to fill your home with a variety of plants, herbs, and fresh-cut flowers.

Positive Talking

It is easy to slip into saying self-deprecating statements, even in moments when you might want to practice self-love and self-compassion. Sometimes you may practice negative self-talk in order to push yourself to grow, acknowledge that you are feeling low, or attempt to humble yourself. But the more you speak negatively about yourself, the more negative you can feel. Notice when you say negative things, such as "I can't . . ." or "I don't . . .," and instead substitute more positive language, such as "I can . . ." and "I will . . .". Think about a time when you said something negative about yourself, and use the space that follows to practice shifting your language to positive self-talk. How would you talk to yourself now to inspire yourself and lift yourself up?

_____

_____

_____

"You are the one who possesses the keys to your being. You carry the passport to your own happiness." —DIANE VON FURSTENBERG

Find Joy in Yourself

We all have interests or hobbies that allow us to unwind, relax, and feel happy or joyful. These hobbies can be a part of your coping toolbox and bring fulfillment. Write down the top three interests or hobbies that bring you joy.

1. _____

2. _____

3. _____

Reflect on Joy

Reflect on specific times when you felt joy and positivity when with friends or family, at school or work, or while traveling, and think about the details of these events that brought on feelings of happiness. Use the following chart to consider the details of the events and the exact positive feelings you felt, as well as the intensity of those feelings.

Details of the Event	Positive Feeling	Intensity
With family or friends		1 2 3 4 5 6 7 8 9 10
School or work		1 2 3 4 5 6 7 8 9 10
Travel		1 2 3 4 5 6 7 8 9 10
Your choice:		1 2 3 4 5 6 7 8 9 10

Recognize the Good

It's important to be reminded, especially in moments when happiness might feel out of reach or a little elusive, of the success of your hard work and what you've achieved. When you need a happiness boost, notice the reminders of the good you have done: awards, diplomas, artwork, letters from loved ones, trophies, photos of milestones, and so on. Whenever you're setting up or reorganizing your environment, such as an office or common space, be sure to include these reminders on the walls, desk, or anywhere you might come across them, and feel inspired by them. Think about the visual reminders of your accomplishments, achievements, and fond memories that you can integrate into your space to make room for more happiness, and make notes in the following space.

_____

_____

_____

Balancing the Negative

Negative thoughts, while often unwelcome, are natural and normal and will still appear from time to time, even when you do your best to focus on the good. When negative thoughts try to challenge the way you think and your coping tools don't feel like the best match for them, the simple act of writing down a negative thought can help let it out and restore your ability to focus on other things. Use the following space to write out some negative thoughts you may be sitting with today as a means to process them. After you've written each thought down and rated its intensity on a scale from 1 to 10, allow the negative thought to cross your mind once more, and notice how you feel this time. Rate your feelings once again to see if your emotions are more balanced now.

Feeling: _____

Intensity: 1   2   3   4   5   6   7   8   9   10

_____

_____

Feeling: _____

Intensity: 1   2   3   4   5   6   7   8   9   10

_____

_____

What Went Well

Think about something that went well recently, such as making progress on an important project. Consider why it went well, whether it was the time, energy, or effort that you put into it, the support you received from peers, or the inspiration that struck. By identifying reasons that are linked specifically to what *you* have done to foster that positive event, you gain agency in experiencing more positivity. List some things that have resulted in some positivity and consider the reasons you were able to make them happen.

What went well?

I made progress on my paper, and I finished my draft.

_____

_____

What specifically did you do to result in it happening?

Because I dedicated a week to working on it and prioritized writing, I was able to make progress.

_____

_____

Finding the Silver Lining

There is great comfort to be found in silver linings, sometimes even feelings of happiness. Consider a recent situation in which you encountered stress, hardship, or discomfort but also discovered a silver lining. How did that silver lining make you ultimately feel? List some of the hardships that come to mind using a keyword or brief phrase and reflect on the silver lining that came from it. Focus on the relief, encouragement, beauty, or joy that the silver lining brought you.

_____

_____

_____

Scheduling Positive and Meaningful Activities

Scheduling positive activities for the near future is a great way to embrace more joy in your life. Holding yourself to these commitments, whether you plan for them to be social or solitary, is crucial in order to access the benefits. The activity can be positive or meaningful, or both. Examples include volunteering at an animal shelter or nursing home, visiting a museum, taking a hike, and spending time with friends. No matter the specific activity, it should bring you some joy.

Personal Experiments

As you make progress in examining the good that is around you, it's also important to reflect on and examine the good within you. When you look inward, avoid being self-critical as best you can. While self-criticism can push you to challenge yourself, you need to be careful not to let it hold you back or make you think poorly of yourself. It can close you off to problem solving. Think back to times in which you motivated yourself through self-criticism versus kinder ways such as self-compassion. Note which times you felt more productive and happier.

Thought	Self-Criticism or Self-Compassion (Critical/Compassion)	Motivating (Yes/No)	Level of Productivity (1 2 3 4 5)
Example: *I'm a failure.*	Critical	No	1
Example: *This is hard, but I can work hard.*	Compassion	Yes	3

Thought Records

Thought records are a great way to track how you can transform your thinking patterns into positive thinking. Through this exercise you will learn the tools to identify the cognitive distortion you engage in and to challenge those distortions and engage in more positive thinking. The bolded entries in the "Cognitive Distortion" column are the ones that apply to the example; highlight or circle the applicable distortions that apply to your own entries.

Event/Trigger	Automatic Negative Thought	Cognitive Distortion	Alternative Thought
Example: *I missed a deadline.*	*I'm a failure. I will get fired. I'm worthless.*	• **All-or-nothing thinking** • Blaming self or others • **Catastrophizing** • **Jumping to conclusions** • **Magnifying the negative** • Minimizing the positive • Overgeneralizing • "Should" statement • Taking things personally	*I made progress on my work even if I didn't meet the deadline. I worked really hard, and I can find productive ways to problem-solve.*
		• All-or-nothing thinking • Blaming self or others • Catastrophizing • Jumping to conclusions • Magnifying the negative • Minimizing the positive • Overgeneralizing • "Should" statement • Taking things personally	

(Continued)

Thought Records (*Continued*)

Event/Trigger	Automatic Negative Thought	Cognitive Distortion	Alternative Thought
		• All-or-nothing thinking • Blaming self or others • Catastrophizing • Jumping to conclusions • Magnifying the negative • Minimizing the positive • Overgeneralizing • "Should" statement • Taking things personally	
		• All-or-nothing thinking • Blaming self or others • Catastrophizing • Jumping to conclusions • Magnifying the negative • Minimizing the positive • Overgeneralizing • "Should" statement • Taking things personally	

CONCLUSION

In this chapter, you explored ways to focus on the good and reframe your thinking to acknowledge accomplishments, create a more uplifting environment, and engage in activities you enjoy. By uncovering and interrupting your negative thought patterns, you can reframe your thinking toward more positivity, which enables you to feel happier each day. When you feel more positive, you will engage with the world in more positive ways. In turn, the world engages with you in more positive ways, and through this feedback loop, you become happier. The next chapter will consider ways that connecting with others will help you embrace more happiness in your life.

SIX
CONNECT WITH OTHERS

Connecting with others can foster feelings of happiness; meaningful connections can help you feel both happier and less stressed. Through these prompts and exercises, you will explore the positive relationships you have in your life, ways to increase social interactions, and methods to develop new relationships. You will also delve into techniques for coping with challenging relationships. Positive interactions with others will increase your prosocial, or positive, behaviors, making you feel more fulfilled. In this chapter, by focusing on your connections with others, you will continue to build on your skills to shift and challenge your automatic negative thought patterns and continue your journey toward happiness.

> "Friendship is unnecessary, like philosophy, like art, like the universe itself . . . It has no survival value; rather it is one of those things which give value to survival." —C. S. LEWIS

REASONS TO BE WITH OTHERS

Being consciously aware of the specific reasons why you want to be around other people or connect with certain people comes about more readily when you foster deeper relationships. Through this exercise you will gain a deeper understanding of your motivation to maintain these relationships. For instance, being with a particular friend might mean you have more courage to go on adventurous outings, or being with a particular family member might provide you with emotional support. In the converse, what qualities do you offer to others in your relationships? By thinking about the reasons you connect with others, you are recognizing and naming the positivity you feel.

- **Why do you connect with others? Are you a person who tends to offer support? Do you tend to solve problems alone? Consider rewarding times in which you have connected with others. Check the reasons you seek out connections and indicate whether there is a specific person you seek out for these things.**

    ❏ **Help others** _____

    ❏ **Receive support** _____

    ❏ **Problem-solving** _____

    ❏ **Spend leisure time together** _____

    ❏ **Explore new places together** _____

    ❏ **Complete daily and/or tedious task** _____

    ❏ **Find support to manage stressors** _____

    ❏ **Other:** _____ _____

Caring for Others

Caring for others can be fulfilling and can enhance your ability to care for yourself, too. Use this space to think of people, animals, or plants you can support or organizations you can join to give to others.

_____

_____

Navigating Stressful Relationships

Encountering strife in relationships is perfectly normal, if not inevitable. There may be specific individuals who bring you stress or components of relationships that cause stress. It's important to identify what about the relationship brings you stress and see if there is a way to reduce it, such as distancing yourself. If you can't distance yourself, give yourself the bandwidth to manage the stress of the relationship by using some of the tools you have for coping. Think about these grounding tools and how they can help you to navigate stressful relationships.

- **Breathing**

- **Going for a walk**

- **Taking space**

- **Engaging in a hobby**

- **Taking a sip of water**

- **Using a distraction**

- **Engaging in humor**

- **Taking a bath**

Open Up to Others

Emotionally connecting with others helps decrease levels of stress and anxiety. Opening up to other people may make you feel vulnerable, especially at first, so consider how to make yourself a person to whom others can open up—that way you can become more familiar and comfortable with this skill. You can do this by listening empathetically and in a nonjudgmental way, and then reflecting on what you hear. As you offer this support to others, you may find that your desire and ability to open up increases. Consider the different people to whom you currently go or could go to talk about the various stressors in your life. Or consider the people you enjoy supporting. Write down three people in your life to whom you can open up or who can open up to you.

Stress *Examples: work, decision-making*	With whom can you connect?

Relationship Quality, Not Quantity

It's not necessarily the quantity of relationships, but the quality of relationships, that can bring you happiness as you fine-tune your relationship circle over time. Having a few good friendships is more meaningful than having a large number of friends who are emotionally distant. Surrounding yourself with deeper relationships where there is a connection through sharing, creating, or supporting one another can outweigh having a countless number of connections founded on a more superficial basis.

Connections for Motivation

Connecting with others can help you stay motivated, especially when you're struggling to find the drive to complete a task. For instance, exercising with friends can help you stay committed to working out. Consider goals you'd like to work toward or activities you have a hard time sustaining, and find a way to make them about connection. You could join a book club, create a study group, or invite friends to help out with home projects. What are some things you would like to accomplish? How can you make them social? When you feel motivated, you are able to engage in inspiring, fulfilling things, which will ultimately help you feel more happiness.

Project or activity	How to make it social
_____	_____
_____	_____
_____	_____

Traditions

Traditions are prescribed cultural frameworks for connecting with people. We use traditions to help us celebrate occasions like holidays and birthdays. We also use them to help us through more difficult times like the loss of a loved one. They provide us with a way to process, connect, bolster ourselves, and find support during these times. Take a moment to reflect on the specifics of some of the traditions you practice and why these acts may bring a sense of positivity, joy, and connection with others and your culture.

Example: Baking for Thanksgiving helps me feel connected to my grandmother.

1. _____

2. _____

3. _____

Let the Past Go

You may have had a past experience with people that left you with lingering feelings of guilt, anger, or resentment. You may wish for a different connection or for circumstances to change. No matter the status of the relationship, letting the feelings of guilt, anger, or resentment go can help you move through challenging memories to develop a different and more compassionate understanding. Consider the feelings that come about when you think about your history with an important person in your life and give yourself some self-compassion as you let the past go.

Feeling	Thought	New Thought/ Self-Compassion

> "If you don't like the road you're walking, start paving another one." —DOLLY PARTON

Social Media

Social media can be a great way to connect with others by finding new interest groups or building on existing relationships. Ideally, you will be able to bring relationships beyond social media connections to in-person connections. Whether you use social media occasionally or constantly, fill your social media with positivity, whether that means following groups with encouraging messages about happiness and self-growth, using online connections to motivate you, or connecting with people who inspire you. You can also make a point to censor anything online that brings about feelings of self-doubt or negativity. Consider your various social media outlets, your feeds, and how you can include more positivity and make more positive connections.

Social Media Outlets Feeds	Feeds	Groups/Follow
Instagram	Negative	Unfollow influencers; Follow Positive Psychology

Making Reconnections

Reconnecting with old friends can bring more positivity to your life by allowing you to share and connect with people who hold knowledge of your past and already know a lot about you. Therefore, connecting with a childhood, high school, or college friend with whom you had a positive relationship and haven't been in touch can be rewarding. With whom in your past can you reconnect who conjures up positive memories? How can you connect with them? Use the space to brainstorm people with whom you may have lost touch and wish to reconnect on your happiness journey.

_____

_____

_____

Scheduling Regular Social Activities

Scheduling regular activities with friends and family can help you push yourself to be more connected with others, and social expectations can help you uphold the commitment you've made to engage. Regularity helps you continue to deepen these relationships and allows you the opportunity to build a reciprocal relationship to open up to one another. Furthermore, collaborating on planning an activity can bring you closer to someone you care about. Consider scheduling something with someone on a regular basis. The activity can be weekly, biweekly, or monthly—any frequency that feels doable and enjoyable.

Who?	Possible Activities	Frequency

How Much Do You Depend on Others?

Determining how dependent or independent you are can help you understand when you need to turn to others for support. By knowing what you need from others, you can seek the type of support that you require, and you will feel more fulfilled in your relationships. Take the following true or false quiz to gain a sense of how much you depend on others. Do not overthink your responses; just answer with the first thought that comes to you. There's no wrong answer.

1. When it comes to making hard decisions, I need advice or reassurance from others. **True / False**

2. It's easier to go along with others than disagree with them. **True / False**

3. I prefer to start projects with the help of others. **True / False**

4. I need approval or assurance from others. **True / False**

5. I prefer the company of others rather than being alone. **True / False**

6. I turn to others to make major life decisions. **True / False**

7. I blame myself if bad things happen. **True / False**

8. I will let people down if I don't fulfill my expectations. **True / False**

9. I am fluid and flexible with most people and can mostly go with the flow.
True / False

If you answered mostly "True," you are a person who needs others around you.
The "True" answers indicate your need to be with others, and you may need more
social connection in order to feel fulfilled.

If you answered mostly "False," you are fairly independent. You are a person who
appreciates time thinking on your own.

If your "True" and "False" answers are fairly evenly split, then you are balanced
between depending on others and relying on yourself. You navigate some issues
with the support of others, while you are able to navigate other times autonomously.

How Do I Enjoy Connections with Others?

There are many ways in which you can enjoy connecting with people, such as
common values and aspirations, coming together over shared interests, building
relationships through novel experiences, or maintaining relationships through similar
comforts. Explore the following categories to determine how you prefer to connect
with others to enhance your sense of connection and fulfillment in your relationships. Note that you may find joy connecting to others in all of these ways. Notice if
there is one particular way you most enjoy and determine with whom you enjoy
connecting in this way so that you can be more intentional in your relationship
with them.

1. Conversations regarding values   **Yes / No**

2. Scheduled and planned events   **Yes / No**

3. Sharing goals together   **Yes / No**

4. Playing games together   **Yes / No**

5. Connecting through similar interests and hobbies   **Yes / No**

6.	Trying new foods	**Yes / No**
7.	Creating things together	**Yes / No**
8.	Exploring new places	**Yes / No**
9.	Sharing everyday moments	**Yes / No**
10.	Celebrating accomplishments	**Yes / No**
11.	Going on an adventure	**Yes / No**
12.	Enjoying regular routines	**Yes / No**

These means of connecting are not mutually exclusive, and you may find that you wish to connect with people in several meaningful ways. Read on to find the meaning behind your answers, and then identify a person with whom you can build or have built this type of connection.

- **If you answered "Yes" to items 1, 3, and 10, then you look to deepen your relationship through shared *values* and *aspirations*. With whom can you share your values and aspirations?** _____

- **If you answered "Yes" to items 4, 5, and 7, then you look to connect through *common interests* and *leisure activities*. With whom can you share your interests and engage in activities?** _____

- **If you answered "Yes" to items 6, 8, and 11, then you thrive on relationships that build on *novelty* and *excitement*. With whom can you explore the world and experience excitement?** _____

- **If you answered "Yes" to items 2, 9, and 12, then you enjoy maintaining relationships through *comforts*. With whom can you experience everyday comforts and routines?** _____

Surround Yourself with Positive Connections

We have all different kinds of relationships in our lives: family, friends, spouses, colleagues, peers, and so on. Consider the relationships that bring you positivity. These can be with people with whom you have significant relationships, like siblings or romantic partners, or people with whom you are acquainted, like your mail carrier or neighbor. Consider how these relationships bring positivity into your life, whether it is small gestures of kindness, a smile, or deeper-rooted connections of joy like sharing interests, values, and goals. No matter the level of the connection, be conscious and present in the feelings of the connection. Who brings you positivity? How do you engage with them? How can you increase your frequency of interactions with them? Use the following chart to map out these positive connections.

Who?	Sense of Positivity (1 2 3 4 5 6 7 8 9 10)	How Can I Increase Our Interaction?

Finding Social Spaces to Enjoy

A wonderful and easy way to tap into happiness is to spend more time in public spaces and witness the natural joy of the world. You don't necessarily need to engage with others, but going to a park, café, or library to read, sip coffee, daydream, or people-watch is a wonderful way to absorb the social world. What are some places you can visit to feel more integrated into the social world? Check the ones that would work.

- ❏ **Park**
- ❏ **Library**
- ❏ **Gym**
- ❏ **Coffee shop**
- ❏ **Museum**
- ❏ **Gallery**
- ❏ **Mall**
- ❏ **Hiking trail**
- ❏ **Shopping district**
- ❏ **Other:** _____

The Spectrum of an Introvert ← → Extrovert

Are you the type of person who turns to the outer world, or are you a person who tends to turn inward? Introversion and extroversion exist on a spectrum; people are not necessarily completely one extreme or the other. But knowing your leanings, like if you are a person who prefers to socialize in larger groups versus more intimate gatherings, can help you determine the ways in which you want to connect with others in order to feel more comfortable, less anxious, and happier during the process. How do you see yourself on this spectrum?

1. I am talkative.   **Yes / No**

2. I prefer to keep to myself.   **Yes / No**

3. I need to decompress after a social gathering.   **Yes / No**

4. I feel energized after a large event.   **Yes / No**

5. I enjoy attention or being in the spotlight.   **Yes / No**

6. I prefer to take in what's going on.   **Yes / No**

7. I enjoy being with several people.   **Yes / No**

8. I enjoy being with a few close friends.   **Yes / No**

9. I express myself better when I'm one-on-one.   **Yes / No**

10. I feel inspired by being around a lot of other people.   **Yes / No**

11. I do not mind being with a larger group of people.   **Yes / No**

12. I often prefer to only be with one or two friends.   **Yes / No**

Give yourself a point if you answered "Yes" to questions 1, 4, 5, 7, 10, or 11.

←---→

Introvert   Extrovert

0   1   2   3   4   5

Strategies to Connect with Others

If you're feeling ready to reach out to others, whether through reconnections or new relationships, but need some strategies to help jump-start the process, you can always connect through a common and relatable story. Sharing a story about yourself to disclose a relatable experience lets someone learn a little about you and feel more connected to you. Let the relationship naturally unfold from there and be willing to walk through any discomfort that may inevitably come with building new relationships. You may find yourself organically cultivating a happy new connection. On the following lines, brainstorm a story or two that you can share as a means to deepen a connection with someone.

Social Experiment

Getting out with friends or building new relationships can feel daunting and over-whelming at first, but there's so much potential to feel rewarded for your efforts; the more you connect with people in person, the more positive feelings you will experience. Consider an experiment the next time you connect with friends.

Activity Engaged/ Considered with Others	Did You Go? (Yes/No)	What Prevented You from Engaging or Motivated You to Engage?	Feeling?
Going out to dinner	*No*	*I had a hard time committing to plans and was worried about engaging in conversation.*	*Lonely, disappointed*
Going to the movies	*Yes*	*Movies put less social pressure on me, and it was a movie I wanted to see.*	*Connected, happy*

Turn Self-Consciousness into a Focus on Others

It's natural to feel nervous and self-conscious when connecting with others. Often, this feeling is unnecessary, though, as your self-conscious thoughts may be coming from your automatic negative thoughts. It's worth it to catch these thoughts as they arise and instead focus on the other person by actively and empathetically listening. Think back to a recent time when you were in a social setting and feeling self-conscious. Note the thought that appeared in that moment and the ways you might have used those thoughts as a reminder to focus more on the person you were with. This exercise can help you be more aware of self-conscious thoughts and actively change them into something more productive.

Self-Conscious Thought	← *transform* →	Focusing on Others
Do I sound stupid when I talk?	← →	*Let me actively listen to my boss.*
I'm not sure if my friend thinks I really care.	← →	*I will reflect back what my friend is saying.*
_____	← →	_____

Growing Your Social Network

Growing your number of social connections can be challenging, but it is worth it. By increasing your social contact, you can form new and deeper relationships, which will lead to greater happiness. One way to connect with more people is by joining a gym, club, sport, interest group, or class to establish new relationships and increase in-person contact with others who have similar interests. People with whom you share an interest or hobby may align with you in more ways than one. What interests do you have that can help you to be more social? Do you have a skill you'd like to develop and know of a group you can join to do so? What groups, centers, facilities, or clubs can you join to nurture an interest?

Whether it's learning a new sport like tennis, gaining a new skill like woodworking, or joining a regular yoga class, you can always use a personal interest as a means to connect with others. Everyday social connections with others, no matter the depth of the relationship, have proven benefits for your mental health and sense of happiness.

Sociability Is Like a Muscle

Social skills are like a muscle: We need to work out with interactions and social feedback to build our sociability strength. If you have been less engaged with others for a while, you may notice some social awkwardness as you start to rebuild this "strength." But because social skills are like a muscle, the more you engage with others, the more you will regain these skills.

Socializing with a novel group of people that has an established way of being with one another, such as being a new member in a book club or starting a new job with new coworkers, might feel daunting, but with continued interactions, you will learn the subtleties of the group and feel more comfortable and confident with its members. Give yourself grace if you find certain connections more challenging or uncomfortable, because you may need some time to work this muscle. With continued effort in connecting, you will find it easier to make meaningful and happy connections.

> I am learning more about myself so I can build more quality relationships with other people and develop a social life that is fulfilling and joyful for me. I will focus on positive relationships in order to embrace more happiness.

CONCLUSION

Social connections can bring us happiness. After all, we are biologically designed to be social beings and thrive on connecting with others. In this chapter, you explored ways to build on social connections, deepen existing relationships, initiate new relationships, and manage stressful ones. As you continue to practice these new skills, consider where you are socially: Are you trying to meet new friends or tighten your existing social circles? Are you trying to deepen your current relationships? Once you know this about yourself, you can consciously pursue and practice the skills that fit your current needs. No matter your situation, you can push yourself to make your social relationships more fulfilling so that you can experience more happiness with others.

PART THREE

Invest in Your Happiness

In this third part of the book, you will continue to explore ways to invite happiness into your life with the goal of establishing a more long-term relationship with this emotion. You will learn how to form new positive habits by setting motivating, achievable goals. As you progress through these pages, I encourage you to acknowledge your growth, take pride in your effort, and celebrate your achievements. Feel free to return to previous chapters to see how far you have come and gain a clearer sense of how you plan to continue to grow and allow more positivity to enter your life. In chapters 7, 8, and 9, you will dive into how happiness is integral to the physical body and ways to respond mindfully to the environment. You will then shift your thoughts to support a brighter, happier future. These chapters will deepen your relationship with happiness and ensure that you've fostered a long-term relationship with positivity in your life.

SEVEN

HEAL YOUR BODY

Our bodies and minds are inherently intertwined, so much so that our physical health directly affects our mental health and vice versa. Physical activities like exercise or leisurely walks can help increase the number of endorphins, or "feel-good" neurochemicals, that flood our brains. Additionally, our bodies provide us with clues as to how we experience stress, so it's important to tune in and address any changes or ailments when they arise. Some examples include poor sleep, muscle tension, and body aches. Decreasing stress will help you function better mentally and physically; for example, stress negatively affects your quality of sleep. In this chapter, you will explore ways to combat physical pain, difficulty sleeping, or fatigue. If you listen to your body and increase your physical movement in approachable and routinized ways, you will feel better and, ultimately, happier.

Jump-start Your Day

There are so many ways you can begin a new day, and moving is a fantastic option. Jump-start your day through physical activity to get your heart rate up and stimulate yourself to feel engaged and ready for anything. Doing small repetitions of cardio after you wake up can also help you battle fatigue. Consider the following movements and check the exercises that might work for you. Try 5 to 10 reps to get your blood pumping and welcome in those endorphins.

- ❏ **Jumping jacks**
- ❏ **Stretching your arms up to the sky**
- ❏ **Touching your toes**
- ❏ **Burpees**
- ❏ **Lunges**

Physically Relax

It's so important to find ways to relax throughout the day—whether you take time to enjoy a cup of tea, observe what's happening outside your window, or go on a refreshing walk. The simple act of stretching to break up your day or spending five minutes to thoughtfully transition between tasks can address your body's needs. More significant breaks in the day, such as taking a warm bath or shower, are another way to physically address your body's need for relaxation. You will find it so rewarding to attune to your body and give it what it needs in order to embrace more positivity into your life. Check activities on this list that you may be able to fold into your day and expand the list with other ideas you have used in the past.

- ❏ **Regular stretching**
- ❏ **Sips of water throughout the day**
- ❏ **Sipping tea**
- ❏ **Taking a bath or shower**
- ❏ **Sitting on a yoga ball**

_____

_____

_____

Consider Your Diet

Much like the benefits of regular, restful sleep and routine physical activity, a healthy diet can also have a positive influence on your mental health. One easy way to improve your diet is to make sure you eat at times that respond to your body's needs; for example, some may need three meals a day, and others may need to eat smaller portions five times a day. Keeping track of the types of foods that enter your body is a great way to ensure that your diet is balanced and nutrient-rich. If you're able to cook at home more often, that's wonderful, too, as doing so supports a healthy and conscious relationship to the food you take into your body. As a happy bonus, the act of cooking can improve your mood. Check the statement that most accurately describes you to find out more about how you may feel about your eating habits.

❑ **I deeply consider my diet and appreciate what I take into my body.**

❑ **I consider my diet, and when I'm able to, I consider what I put into my body.**

❑ **I do not have the ability to improve my diet.**

❑ **I often give in to my indulgences and find myself taking in foods that might not be very healthy.**

If you endorsed statement 1 or 2, you may already engage in healthy eating habits. If you endorsed statement 3, change may be challenging currently, so give yourself grace, try your best to be more conscious of what you take in, and consider when change is more appropriate for your life. If you endorsed statement 4, you may be ready to change as you recognize that you're engaging in some unhealthy habits that aren't serving you best. Set some small, achievable goals, such as substituting one meal a week with something more nutritious and slowly increasing your intake of healthier foods.

Diet and Mood

A healthy diet can support your mental health and well-being and offset symptoms of depression and anxiety. Your diet and mood are bidirectionally related; your mood affects the foods you choose to eat, and the foods you choose to eat affect your mood. For instance, feeling anxious leads to eating more carbs, which leads to sudden peaks and dips in blood sugar levels, which result in more symptoms of anxiety. Moreover, the microbiome in your gut interacts with your brain and affects your neural, inflammatory, and hormonal systems. Adherence to diets like those eaten in the Mediterranean can help with mood and with food choices.

Notice Your Surroundings to Improve Your Sleep

A regular, healthy, and restful sleep is also affected by your environment, which is why reducing stressful triggers in your bedroom is crucial to improving your sleep. Do you have visual reminders of professional duties in your room? Distracting clutter? How can you keep your bedroom as stress-free and relaxing as possible?

_____

_____

_____

_____

I am developing new healthier habits around my diet and exercise in order to embrace a happier me because my body and mind are integrated.

Journal or Checklist

When you hold worries in your mind, putting them down can be difficult; it often feels like it's your duty to perseverate and tend to these anxieties or fears. Keeping a pencil and a notebook on your nightstand can be a helpful way to externalize the worries; once you write them down, you know they will be held for you on the pages. Often, a quick checklist or to-do list of the thoughts that keep you up at night can help you put these worries aside. Give this a try now by jotting down examples of the thoughts that appear in your mind before you go to bed.

- _____
- _____
- _____
- _____
- _____
- _____

A Walk

A walk outdoors sounds so simple, and yet it can be so successful in shifting your mood. Moving through outdoor green spaces supports mental health and helps reset stuck or negative thought patterns. If walking outdoors isn't possible, you can always try walking on a treadmill indoors while looking at a favorite image of the outdoors. If you're able to engage in regular walking, where would you enjoy walking on a regular basis?

- ❏ **At the park**
- ❏ **In my neighborhood**
- ❏ **On a walking trail**
- ❏ **In my home**
- ❏ **Other:** _____

Stressful Aches and Pains

Don't ignore your body. Physical aches and pains can be a source of stress *and* can come from stress. Note if you carry stress in your arms, legs, back, neck, or head. By knowing how stress physically affects you, you can begin to take action to address the physical aches through stretching, massage, muscle relaxation, or other methods. Minimizing the aches and pains will, in turn, lower the stress caused by them. Where in your body do you tend to feel aches and pains?

Exercise Literally

It's so important to find engaging ways to move your body in order for physical exercise to support mental health. Answer these questions to determine whether you need to adjust your exercise type and amount, and how you could increase your experience of the happy benefits of moving.

What kinds of exercise do you or would you like to engage in? *(running, bicycling, working out at the gym, hiking, etc.)*

_____

_____

_____

How often do you exercise?

❑ **Never**

❑ **Once a week**

❑ **Twice a week**

❑ **Every other day**

❑ **Daily**

How would you like to change your exercise?

- ❏ **Begin a workout routine.**

- ❏ **Increase my duration (length of workouts).**

- ❏ **Increase the frequency (number of times per week).**

- ❏ **I already work out often and feel satisfied with my routine as it brings me a way to address stress.**

Now that you have answered these questions, do you feel that you should add a variety of exercises to your routine? Or should you increase the time or duration of your exercise? The first step to engaging with exercise differently is identifying what you want to do differently.

Physically Mapping Your Stress

In the body, stress is related to the release of cortisol and adrenaline and the activation of the sympathetic system, or the fight-or-flight system. Our bodies evolved to survive during regular threats to our lives; however, we currently don't need to respond to stress in the way that our bodies are designed to. Instead, being conscious that your body reacts in this manner to stressful situations is helpful. When you are feeling stressed, you may notice the physical symptoms or that you have less patience, are being short with your loved ones, and are yelling more. How can you pause, breathe, and then shift your reactions to more measured responses?

Reaction		**Coping**		**Response**
(Yelling)		*(Breathing)*		*(Speaking)*
_____	→	_____	→	_____
_____	→	_____	→	_____
_____	→	_____	→	_____
_____	→	_____	→	_____

Develop a Healthy Diet

A healthy diet can support your mood. Eating healthy fats, incorporating fruits and vegetables, eating high-fiber meals, and limiting junk food can fuel your body, reduce your stress, improve your overall physical health, and help you think better. How can you foster a healthier diet, whether that means cooking more, limiting takeout or fast food, or being more conscientious about balancing your meals?

Yoga

Yoga is beneficial for the body because it improves strength and flexibility, helps you engage in diaphragmatic breathing, and incorporates meditation into the practice. Yoga is fairly accessible through free online videos, or you can sign up for an in-person class. If you haven't tried yoga before, what skills and results would you like to gain from the practice? If you're currently practicing yoga, how can you make it a more important part of your routine that ushers in feelings of peace and happiness?

Where	**How**	**Frequency**
(Home, studio)	*(Class, online streaming)*	*(Weekly, monthly)*
_____	_____	_____
_____	_____	_____
_____	_____	_____
_____	_____	_____

Goal Ladder

It's important to set realistic goals for yourself at every stage of your happiness journey. Ensuring that you are setting attainable goals can motivate you to continue to grow as you tackle shifts in your diet, exercise, and sleep, all of which are challenging. Thoughtfully modifying your goals throughout the process is key to growth, and celebrating your progress as you attain even the smallest achievement can motivate you.

Imagine your self-growth as a ladder with many rungs from top to bottom, representing changing your diet, increasing exercise, regulating sleep, or any combination of the three. How can the rungs of your ladder help break up your aspirations into incremental steps of what's immediately attainable?

- _____
- _____
- _____
- _____
- _____

Guided Meditation to Relax

Stress is normal, but having consistently high levels of stress can make you less productive and feel ill at ease throughout the day. So what can you do? Guided meditation, or using auditory and/or visual imagery as a means to begin to meditate, can be helpful to reset your neurochemistry and allow you to feel less stressed. Guided meditations can be found all over the Internet, on podcasts, and through readings. From the following list, choose the type of place you'd like to visualize and give guided meditation a try.

- **The beach**
- **The woods**
- **The mountains**
- **A comfortable room in your home**
- **Your garden or yard**
- **A favorite vacation spot**

"Peace is the result of retraining your mind to process life as it is, rather than as you think it should be." —WAYNE W. DYER

Sleep Hygiene

Your moods affect your sleep. When you are stressed or worried or sad, you may find yourself fatigued during the day or having a tough time falling asleep. In these circumstances, it helps to establish a regular and comforting routine to engage in before you go to bed. Going to bed and waking at regular times can help you set a healthy sleep rhythm. Engaging in other regular rituals prior to going to bed, such as aromatherapy, drinking a calming tea, reading, or meditation, can also encourage and enhance sleep. Falling asleep more easily can ultimately make you feel more refreshed in the morning and eager to take on a new day.

Staying asleep is also an issue for some. If you wake at night, avoid exposure to screens; rather, mentally prepare yourself by expecting yourself to wake, and set up a ritual for this time as well, like listening to a guided meditation or engaging in progressive relaxation. Use this space to jot down a few ideas that could support you falling asleep and staying asleep.

_____

_____

_____

Recreational Physical Activities

Playing sports or other recreational activities can bring joy and peace to your life. When you experience pleasure from these activities, you can pave yet another avenue to happiness. Do you engage in any activities like squash, golf, tennis, or swimming? Consider the recreational activities you engage in and think about how they foster feelings of positivity, a joyful link between your physical body and your mental state.

_____

_____

_____

Routinize Your Workout

If you're already moving on occasion and feeling the good results, you might be interested in increasing your workouts, getting stronger, and feeling fitter, healthier, and happier. It can be challenging to increase your skills and strengths if you don't work on them consistently. Creating an easy-to-follow routine is a great way to tackle this challenge. Consider setting aside specific days of the week or times of the day for exercise. Use this chart to plan out your new invigorating exercise schedule. Remember to be realistic with your goals and place an "X" when you can exercise.

	Morning	Mid-Day	Evening
Mon			
Tues			
Wed			
Thurs			
Fri			
Sat			
Sun			

Pet Yourself on the Back

For many people, pets are a source of positivity, and they support physical and mental well-being. They promote exercise (walking the dog), bring you physical contact and comfort, decrease feelings of loneliness, and help you feel more positive. Pets are not limited to dogs and cats; birds, lizards, and even fish can offer emotional support as well. The act of caring for a creature can give you purpose and help you better appreciate the smaller joys in life. Do you have a pet? How do your pets enhance your happiness? If you don't have one, would you consider a pet?

How Self-Care Can Activate Your Mirror Neurons

Personal self-care is crucial to having a balanced life as you combat the negativity you may feel and experience. Through self-care you can open yourself up to the positivity that surrounds you in your everyday moments. One way to practice self-care is to tend to your physical appearance; how you dress or make up yourself for the day influences your mood. Interestingly, you can physically put yourself together when you don't feel "put together" to jump-start your brain to invite more happiness through the activation of mirror neurons. Mirror neurons are neurons that live in the brain and can activate emotional states when we witness an event, like when we experience joy while watching an uplifting movie. By creating an appearance that makes you happy, you can activate your mirror neurons to start to feel happy. Engage in self-care and invest in your personal appearance to bring more happiness into your life.

Physical Movement to Promote Social Interaction

Getting active with other people has so many benefits. It can inspire and motivate you, and it can help you reach a physical exercise goal. Engaging in a physical activity with friends or family or as part of a class will simply help you to exercise more. How can you remain physically active with others?

_____

_____

_____

_____

In Moderation!

Drinking alcohol is not necessarily a positive coping tool because it lets you escape various issues rather than addressing them and coping with them in effective ways. It's important to be conscious of the reasons you drink or use drugs and how substances can work against your body and mind. Check any statements that describe you.

❑ **I find myself drinking or using substances as a means to cope with stress.**

❑ **Others have been concerned with my drinking and/or substance use.**

❑ **I've tried to reduce my drinking/substance use but found it challenging.**

❑ **I often feel hung over after I drink or use substances.**

❑ **I have neglected some responsibilities due to my drinking or drug use.**

If you checked any of the preceding items, you may want to consider a new relationship with alcohol or drug use by either reducing or limiting your use. Try setting small, reasonable goals to reduce and adding other ways to cope with stress or worry, like exercise. If reducing is too challenging, seek professional help; there is nothing at all to be ashamed of.

Coping with Stress Pain

Your mood can impact your body, and understanding how and where you carry any feelings of stress, tension, or worry is important in order to heal. Locate where you carry stress in your body. For some, it's a tightening in the chest or a pain in the stomach. For others, it's a tension headache or soreness in the shoulders and neck. Once you are able to locate where you feel your stress, consider ways to release that tension physically through stretches, applying heat, or deep breathing. If the pain is very troublesome, strategies such as acupuncture or massage therapy can also address the discomfort.

| **Where Do I Feel My Stress?** | **How Can I Address My Stress?** |
| | *(Yoga, acupuncture, massage, exercise)* |

❏ **Anxious in my belly** _____

❏ **Headaches** _____

❏ **Tightness in my throat or neck** _____

❏ **Soreness in my back, shoulders, or neck** _____

❏ **Other** _____

Consider How Stress Works for You

Stress is natural and subjective. What causes stress for one may not cause stress for another. Consider why you feel stressed in the first place. Stress directly related to accomplishing a task is actually a motivating agent to help you change: Too little stress doesn't motivate you, and too much stress overwhelms you and may hurt you physically. But just the right (safe and manageable) amount of stress can motivate you to engage in challenging yet fulfilling tasks that support and even enhance your happiness.

For instance, a deadline, upcoming review, and threat of not getting paid are "stresses," or external motivating factors that might get you started on various tasks, and some people need a little "heat under them" in order to get certain tasks completed. Are you the type of person who will start a less enjoyable project once a deadline is put in place?

Fill out the following chart with the various things you do, from pleasurable tasks to tasks that do not interest you. Consider what level of stress gets you motivated to perform certain tasks.

10	**VERY STRESSED**	*Overwhelmed, can't accomplish tasks*
9	**TOO STRESSED**	*Engage in tasks but in an unproductive manner*
8	↑	_____
7		*(e.g., studying for licensure test)*
6		_____
5	**MOTIVATED ZONE**	_____
4		*(e.g., filing taxes)*
3		_____
2	↓	*(e.g., knitting as a new hobby)*
1	**LOW STRESS**	*Will engage in fun hobbies/interests*
0	**NO STRESS**	*Underwhelmed and not motivated*

Starting to Feel the Tension

Being aware of the general pattern of how stress develops in your body and knowing where you physically feel the tension will help you successfully manage these times. When you notice tension in your body throughout the day, try to engage in breathing: Inhale and notice the tension, and then let out a long exhale that releases the tension through your breath. Try this five times. In the following space, jot down when you notice stress appear, where, and how you feel after engaging in a breathing exercise.

_____

_____

_____

Progressive Relaxation

Scanning your body from head to toe while releasing tension that exists in your muscles is an accessible, helpful, and effective technique to deal with the times you are fatigued, overwhelmed, sore, or stressed. Follow these steps to try a full-body progressive relaxation. As you try this exercise, notice if there is a particular part of the body that really benefits. You can use this practice throughout the day as you notice stress building, giving you the ability to let it go and allowing you to invite more positive feelings into your body and mind.

As you engage in this practice, know that the first few times may feel unnatural. But don't worry; continue to practice until the muscle progression is ritualized and you don't need to refer to the steps in this workbook. Once you are familiar with the process, you may want to add more stretches to address tension in particular areas. Or you may want to skip over zones of your body to focus on other areas, especially if you have limited time in the day to practice. Ideally, the exercise should take about 15 to 20 minutes.

1. Find a comfortable place to sit or lie down. If you are sitting, plant your feet on the floor and straighten your back against the chair or use pillows for support.

2. Take three to five deep breaths, inhaling through your nose and elongating your exhale. Gently lower your gaze on the exhale (but do not close your eyes), slightly relaxing your neck as you look down.

3. Starting with your toes, flex them up to the sky three times, point them out as your heels are on the ground, and slowly relax your feet so the tops of them feel heavy.

4. Next, move up to your legs, flexing your leg muscles three times. Straighten your legs out and slowly relax them down until your legs feel heavy.

5. Now flex your thigh muscles three times, and every time you relax your muscles, let your thighs feel heavy and supported by your seat.

6. Focus on your glutes, tensing the muscles three times and relaxing them until they feel heavy as well.

7.   Now focus on your core. Gently tighten the muscles and then relax; repeat three times.

8.   Move up to your chest, inhaling and exhaling three times, noticing your breath.

9.   Focusing on your shoulders, lift them and then relax them down at least three times until they feel heavy and relaxed.

10.   Raise your arms up and down to tense them; then lift your hands so your fingertips are pointed up to the sky and relax them down flat again.

11.   Gently roll your neck side to side and all around to release any tension, moving carefully so you don't hurt your neck.

12.   Focusing on your face muscles, make a huge smile and release it down, repeating this a few times. Move up to your eyebrows, raising them as high as they will go and then releasing the tension. (You may feel self-conscious during this step, and that is okay; just notice your self-conscious thoughts and see if you can give yourself some self-compassion.)

13.   Notice the energy you feel at the very top of your head, the highest point of your body, and focus on your breathing once again.

14.   Gently open your gaze when you are ready and bask in how relaxed you feel.

CONCLUSION

You explored the various ways in which your body and mind are interconnected and tried various techniques to address discomforts you may feel as a means to manage stress and invite more happiness into your life. As you progress through the workbook, continue to consider the various exercises that have worked for you and find ways to organically fold these newfound coping tools into your life. As with all the chapters, feel free to revisit the text to give yourself a little boost if you find yourself needing motivation to stay physically attuned. In the next chapter, we will expand on the mind-body connection and dig more deeply into the practice of mindfulness.

EIGHT

RESPOND MINDFULLY

Mindfulness is the act of being present in the moment, taking in your surroundings while attuning to your senses, noticing your mood, and practicing acceptance. Mindful interventions are effective in reducing symptoms of anxiety, depression, fatigue, and chronic pain. As these symptoms decrease, happiness can grow. The act of slowing down and consciously becoming aware of yourself and your environment can help you notice the smaller things in life that bring you joy. This process can help you better appreciate the world you live in—even the little things, such as the warmth from the sunlight or the crispness in the air. You can easily overlook and take for granted these little elements that add up to positive day-to-day experiences. In this chapter you will explore ways to be more present in order to embrace the little joys in life.

Ground Yourself in Your Senses

Noticing your senses can help you begin to practice mindfulness. Some senses, like sight and hearing, are easier to notice because you rely on them heavily to navigate the world. You may need to focus a bit more to notice tastes and smells when you are not actively engaging these senses. Take a moment to write down what you notice from your senses right now. Is there a sense that is more challenging to focus on?

Name three things you see: _____

Name three things you hear: _____

Name two things you feel: _____

Name two things you smell: _____

Name one thing you taste: _____

Attune to Your Body

It's important to know your body, and attuning, or paying attention, is helpful in giving your body what it needs. Attuning to your body is another way to remain more present and grounded within yourself. Use the following checklist to notice the state of your body without judgment.

What is your body temperature?	❏ Warm	❏ Just right	❏ Cool
What's your breathing like?	❏ Fast	❏ Evenly paced	❏ Slow
How do your muscles feel?	❏ Tight	❏ Relaxed	❏ Loose

Set Up 10 Minutes of Daily Mindfulness

Routines are important to ground yourself throughout the day, so setting up a moment to be mindful each day can help you be present and embrace more happiness. Consider ways you can set aside 10 minutes for mindfulness each day.

When can you fold it into your life? *(For example: As part of my evening routine)*

_____

How will you practice being mindful? *(For example: Listening to a guided meditation)*

_____

What Emotions Do You Feel?

We often move throughout the day not fully aware of how we feel and not realizing how our feelings can affect how we act. For instance, if you are tired, you might find yourself acting grumpy toward others. If you are worried, you may find yourself feeling more distracted and less patient with others. It's important to check in with your mood throughout the day. Quickly scan yourself to see how you currently feel and then reflect on what you have felt thus far today.

Currently I feel: _____

Today, I have felt: _____

Combatting Mood Shifts

Your moods shift throughout the day, and several things can move you from a positive place to a negative place. Following these steps can help you combat the various mood shifts throughout the day.

1. Identify the trigger. Knowing what makes you feel a particular emotion is an important first step.

2. Acknowledge the feeling. Your feeling is valid.

3. Let the negativity go. When you are ready to move through the negative emotion, you can engage in one of your coping skills to let it go.

4. Invite the positivity in. Notice something positive in your life, big or small.

Step Outside Your Routine

Having a routine is important because it helps you jump-start your day and close your day with intention and purpose. Yet routine can take you out of mindfulness. As you get routinized in your schedule, you may go into automatic mode and out of the moment itself. Every now and then, shake up your routine slightly to help you be more present and conscious. You could try taking a new route to work or school, or having breakfast before getting dressed. How can you mix up your routine to reset and be more present? Remember that you can always return to the routine that works best for you, but open yourself up to trying something new, if only just for a day.

Current Routine

New Routine

_____

_____

_____

_____

Grounding Techniques to Cope with Stress

Everyone experiences stress from time to time. While you may wish to banish the feeling altogether, it's important to notice the feelings of stress and take a moment to ground yourself through some coping skills. Coping skills like breathing, taking a sip of cold water, taking a movement break, or going for a walk can help you manage little stresses and re-center yourself in the present moment. Consider the various coping tools that can help you ground yourself in the present moment.

- **Sip of water or tea**

- **Taking a walk**

- **Stretching**

- **Quick movement break**

- **Saying a mantra**

- **Placing notes or visual cues around your home**

- **Taking a breath**

- **Petting your dog or cat**

- **Watering a plant**

- **Noticing your senses**

- **Other:**

You are here, in the present moment, setting goals in order to embrace a better, happier you. You are considering the way you think, the way you act, the way you connect, and the way you feel, and noticing all of these things presently. You are mindful of yourself and your life.

Acceptance and Commitment Therapy

Acceptance and commitment therapy, also known as ACT, stems from CBT. ACT focuses on accepting rather that avoiding, denying, or changing internal struggles caused by emotional states. ACT, developed by Steven C. Hayes in 1982, uses mindfulness-based interventions to help individuals normalize and accept challenging or uncomfortable feelings. Some of the interventions include acceptance, which entails accepting an emotion rather than denying or suppressing it; observing self, which involves reflecting on emotions and thoughts while in the moment; cognitive diffusion, which means objectifying experiences; and being present.

By accepting that you can experience uncomfortable feelings during certain situations, you can begin to resist the struggle of trying to force your anxious and depressive symptoms to "go away." The ACT intervention approach embraces psychological flexibility and encourages you to practice being present with your feelings. It can help you improve your mood and embrace more happiness.

Daily Self-Care

Small everyday moments of self-care can help you practice being mindful. Engaging in these moments daily can help flex and build these so-called mindfulness muscles. Think about three daily self-care exercises you can do, and consider how they can help you be more mindful.

- _____
- _____
- _____

Pause with a Breath

Whether you're having a conversation or reading an email, take a moment to pause before you respond. During the pause you can take a breath and quickly scan your body and mood. This will give you the ability to respond with a clear head. Reflect on a situation or event in the recent past when you wish you had taken that breath before responding to someone or something. What response would you have given instead?

Event	Breath	Response
_____	→	_____
_____	→	_____
_____	→	_____

Situations That Drive Your Feelings

Being able to identify specific triggers that elicit certain emotions—whether they are categorically good or bad—is important because it gives you the ability to navigate a situation more effectively. You may find yourself avoiding some situations as a means to prevent negative experiences, which is a way of coping. In the following table, review the feelings named and write down the times when you have felt them. By identifying your triggers and the resultant emotions, you will be more conscious of your experiences and able to deal with the emotions successfully.

Anxious	Arrogant	Bored	Confident	Curious
Determined	Frustrated	Grieving	Guilty	Happy
Hurt	Hopeful	Jealous	Sad	Shy

Guided Mindfulness

Being present is a skill that requires regular practice. Guidance is helpful. Practicing ways to be mindful is easy given the numerous resources—podcasts, books, apps, and websites (many free)—that concentrate on the subject. Which of these guided tools do you use or would you use? Think of ways that you can practice this week using one or more of these tools.

- **Smartphone app**

- **Book**

- **Podcast**

- **Audiobook**

- **Website**

- **Other:** _____

Ground Yourself through a Single Sense

Focusing on just one sense and taking in all the information from that single sense can help you focus in the moment. It can especially help you redirect your focus away from any feelings of sadness, worry, or stress. For this exercise, you will home in on hearing by following the prompts.

- **Notice all the sounds in your body. For example, you may hear yourself breathing or the beating of your heart or a rumbling in your belly. What do you hear in your body?**

  _____

  _____

  _____

- **Notice all the sounds in the room you are in. These could be sounds from different machines or appliances or the ticking of a clock. What noises do you hear in the room?**

  _____

  _____

  _____

- **Notice all of the sounds outside the room. These could be sounds from someone in the next room, the breeze blowing outside, or cars passing by. What do you hear outside the room?**

  _____

  _____

- Now that you have listened to the various sounds in your overall environment, notice if you can hear two sounds simultaneously. What are those two sounds?

_____

_____

_____

- What three sounds can you hear simultaneously?

_____

_____

_____

- Now listen to all the sounds and reflect on how easy or challenging the exercise was. Were you focused or not? If you lost focus, just note what made you lose that focus—no judgment.

_____

_____

Shift Your Feelings

All of the emotions that you experience are valid. During times when your negative emotions feel more consuming, you need to become more present in the moment to take in the situation for what it is versus how it feels, which will help you shift out of the feeling. Practice shifting your feelings by tracking your emotions and integrating coping tools at the same time.

What negative emotion do you recall most vividly?
(Sadness, anger, loneliness, etc.)

_____

Intensity of feelings   1 2 3 4 5 6 7 8 9 10

Circle the coping tools you can use to acknowledge the feeling and move through it to be more present in the moment.

Take five breaths	Take a walk	Drink water	Break for a stretch	Step outside
Take some space	Name the feeling	Notice your senses	Ground yourself with one sense	Water a plant
Connect with a pet	Connect with family or friends	Move physically	Journal	Tidy up (change your environment)

After using one or more coping methods, do you feel the same or different?

_____

Intensity of feeling   1 2 3 4 5 6 7 8 9 10

Where You Feel Your Feelings

Because your emotions activate your visceral motor system, you will often feel your emotions physiologically. Feelings such as fear, anger, happiness, sadness, and surprise can stimulate the system, and you can sense changes in your heart rate and blood flow. When this happens, you might feel flushed or sweaty or have an upset stomach. Identifying where you notice your feelings within your body will help you be more mindful of the connection between body and mind. When you notice the following feelings, where do you tend to feel them in your body?

Emotion	Where in Your Body You Feel It
Anger	
Sadness	
Fear	
Happiness	
Surprise	

Release Your Feelings Physically

As you notice how different feelings sit in your body, you can choose to embrace or shake those feelings. Follow this exercise to try to experience your emotions with mindfulness and gently release the energy that accompanies them.

- **First notice the various feelings you have in your body.**

- **Take note of where in your body you feel the emotion. Describe the sensation.**

- **Take a deep breath in, focusing your breathing on the part of your body that senses the emotion, and exhale out, releasing the energy with your breath.**

- **Notice if there is a shift in the physical sensation of the emotion, take another breath in, and exhale out.**

- **Repeat this method once more, and notice if there is a shift in your feelings. Remember to try this slowly, spending about five to eight minutes on this process.**

Mental Subtraction of a Positive Event

One way to be more mindful is to reflect on a positive past event, mentally "subtracting" that positive event from your personal storyline and then considering the outcome without the positive event. This exercise is inspired by the work of Minkyung Koo and colleagues, who studied how considering the absence of a positive event improves mood and how this can increase positive feelings of these and following events. Reflecting on the fact that the situation may not have occurred helps you appreciate the fact that it did occur. As a result, your positive perceptions of the situation grow and encompass more than just the event itself.

Write about the impact on your life if a positive event that *did* happen hadn't happened. It can be anything, like meeting a significant other, getting a certain opportunity at work, or benefiting from an act of kindness. Does imagining the absence of the event make you appreciate the event more?

_____

_____

_____

_____

React versus Respond

There may not seem to be a major difference between reacting and responding, but they are actually quite different. When you react to a situation, your sympathetic system is activated, so you move quickly, act efficiently, but may behave in a way or say things that you wish you hadn't. When you respond, this process can feel less efficient; you are more conscious of and deliberate about deciding how to behave.

You may find it difficult to reign yourself in so that you are regularly responding rather than reacting to situations. Often, your reactions will be instinctual, and you cannot deny that "gut feeling." By pausing, breathing, and practicing mindfulness, however, you can check to see if your reaction is necessary for the situation and consider whether a different response may be more helpful.

Exploring Your Intentions

Setting an intention, purpose, or goal for the day can help guide you mindfully through that day. Consider your goals as you have embarked on the journey toward more happiness. Are you attempting to take in more of the little moments? Are you working toward a cognitive shift? Do you feel more joy when you connect with others? Have you been able to center yourself by attuning to your body? Checking in with yourself throughout the day by setting up visual reminders or setting a timer can help you be more mindful of the intentions you set forth for the day.

With this reflection in mind, set an intention for yourself, such as *I am going to focus on the little moments to anchor me through the day.*

What is your intention?

_____

_____

Movement and Stillness

You can ground yourself in the present moment through various senses, but you can also do so through body movement. As you move and are still, you are building another way to ground your body, be more present, and ultimately embrace more happiness. Consider where your body is in the moment with no need to change its position.

Note all of the ways your body feels.

_____

_____

In this current position, begin to move around, whether it's a wiggle, a tensing, or a gentle rock or shake, and then make your body completely still. Alternate between movement and stillness for 30 seconds at a time for a total of 2 to 3 minutes. Finish by taking three deep breaths. Are there any changes to how your body feels?

_____

_____

Mindfulness in Your Day

Put together all of the mindfulness skills you've learned—naming your feelings and triggers, deep breathing, focusing on your senses, and attuning to your physical body—while engaging in an everyday activity, like eating, caring for animals or plants, going for a walk, or taking in your environment. Work on being present in the moment, and when your mind drifts off to non-present thinking, remember that's okay. Just use one of the mindfulness techniques to bring yourself back to the moment. Try working up to doing this for 15 minutes. Once you have completed this practice, consider the following reflection questions to help you refine your skills.

What was easy about this practice? _____

How can you build on what came easily to you? _____

What was challenging? _____

How can you address some of these challenges? _____

What thoughts did you notice without judgment? _____

What feelings came up for you? _____

Rate the intensity of these of these
feelings:　　　　　　　　　　　　1　2　3　4　5　6　7　8　9　10

> "Now and then it's good to pause in our pursuit of happiness
> and just be happy." —GUILLAUME APOLLINAIRE

CONCLUSION

Being present, or mindful, can help you embrace the everyday moments in order to notice the little joys of life and feel more positive throughout the day. The act of being mindful is a skill that takes a lot of practice and patience, but you are on your way to mastering the practice. With all of your hard work and dedication throughout this workbook, you now have the tools to grow in this skill.

NINE

ENVISION A BRIGHT FUTURE

This chapter will help you continue to stay focused on your personal journey to achieving happiness. You have explored ways to combat and manage negative thoughts, stress, and negative emotions. You have learned new skills and tools to help keep you physically healthy, mentally grounded, mindful, and focused on your intentions. Now, you will refine these tools and solidify ways to maintain these skills so that they continue to allow you to welcome more joy into your life.

Future Planning

Envisioning plans for the future can help you continue to look forward. These plans can be simple, like scheduling dinners or meeting up with friends. Or they can be larger projects, like a home renovation. Whatever the plans, looking forward to something in the future can inspire feelings of hope and can provide you with opportunities for self-care and respite. What short-term and long-term plans can you make?

The Coping Toolbox

You have worked hard to build your coping toolbox. You may have several helpful tools in there, but perhaps you've found a "go-to" tool that you really trust. Consider your top three coping tools this week and reflect upon the circumstances in which you used them.

1. _____

2. _____

3. _____

Congratulate Yourself!

As you consider ways to maintain your long-term happiness, it is important to congratulate yourself on the progress you've made thus far.

How would you describe your overall mood when you first started this journey?
_____

Which exercises and practices have best fit in your life? _____

Which exercises didn't support your goals? *(It's great to know what doesn't work as well as knowing what does work!)* _____

How do you plan to maintain these skills in your life? _____

Switching Gears

Sometimes, no matter how hard you may be working on noticing your feelings and being present in them, you need to move quickly through them to complete a task or meet a deadline. There are times when distraction from these moments is necessary, such as when working or caring for children. You can always engage in quick and easy coping skills, such as taking a breath or drinking cold water, and then refocusing on the task. Think about some of your preferred go-to coping skills to switch gears quickly.

_____

_____

_____

What Is Your Favorite Time of the Day?

Knowing you have a particular favorite time of the day can help you ground yourself and practice mindfulness at that moment in order to be more present and embrace the small moments of positivity. For some people, this can be the quiet in the morning or the routine of watching the sunset. It can be a time in which you gather with your family or possibly a time you unwind at the end of the day. No matter the time you choose, reflect on your favorite part of the day and how you can practice being present during that time.

Distraction as a Means to Cope

Sometimes, it's challenging or uncomfortable to stay present in our heavier emotions, and we need to distract ourselves in order to cope. Distractions can be any type of positive activity that helps you redirect your negative emotions toward feelings of peace, calm, or happiness. Circle all of the distractions in the following list that have worked for you in the past, and add other types of distractions that you'd like to try next time.

Reading	**Watching an uplifting movie**	**Exercising**	**Connecting with positive people**
Listening to music	**Creating something**	**Gardening**	**Watching an inspiring TV show**
Caring for someone	**Listening to a podcast**	**Taking a walk**	**Cleaning or organizing**
_____	_____	_____	_____

A helpful extra step is to notice the feelings you may have, rate the intensity of the feelings, and reevaluate your feelings and their intensity once again after you've engaged in a positive distraction.

Feeling: _____

Intensity   1   2   3   4   5   6   7   8   9   10

Distraction: _____

Feeling after distraction: _____

Intensity after distraction   1   2   3   4   5   6   7   8   9   10

> " I have also learnt, from experience, that the greater part of our happiness or misery depends upon our dispositions, and not upon our circumstances." —MARTHA WASHINGTON

How Do You Self-Care?

You know that self-care—moments, thoughts, and actions that are calming, relaxing, and restorative—is important and that you define it in your own unique way. Self-care can be as simple as a daily vitamin or as grand as taking a tropical vacation. Consider your favorite methods of self-care and how they can be small, medium, and large in nature and effect.

Self-Care

Small	*Deep breaths*
Medium	*Exercising, gardening*
Large	*Taking a vacation*

Reestablish and Reconsider Your Routines

As you near the end of the workbook, now is a great time to revisit and reestablish the routines you started at the very beginning of this happiness journey. These are the routines that you put into place in the morning and evening, and the ones that reset you as a means to be more present. If there are elements in the routines that have been hard to maintain, consider whether they need to remain. Reflect on the following prompts to reinvigorate your daily rituals.

What is easy about your morning routine?

_____

What is easy about your evening routine?

_____

What were some of the elements that were hard to keep in either of these routines? *(e.g., set wake-up or bedtime)*

_____

Can you reintegrate the challenges in your routine to make them easier, or remove those elements altogether for ease?

_____

About You

It's really powerful to identify attributes that you like about yourself. In the following list, circle all of the characteristics that you like about yourself. Return to this page at a later time if necessary to add more.

Friendly	Serious	Focused	Kind	Generous
Caring	Quiet	Shy	Thoughtful	Insightful
Reserved	Ambitious	Relaxed	Open	Talkative

_____   _____   _____   _____   _____

_____   _____   _____   _____   _____

The Power of Appreciation

Appreciation fosters joyful feelings because it focuses on the positive experiences in life. It helps you consider what you have as opposed to what you desire. Feeling grateful can support your mental health, as seen in a study by Joshua Brown and Joel Wong. In the study, those seeking counseling had better results when they were asked to acknowledge what they were grateful for; the study demonstrated that appreciation not only benefits those who are already well adjusted but can foster more positivity in those who are emotionally struggling. The researchers further found that acknowledging what you are grateful for can help you move from more negative emotions. Noting what you appreciate will not automatically shift your well-being. It does its work over time, so be open to investing that time by noting regularly the things for which you feel grateful.

Affirmations!

Although it can feel strange to say something positive about yourself—perhaps you're very selfless, modest, or shy—doing so can be beneficial. Research has revealed that if you can identify something positive about yourself, you can support yourself in personal growth. Come up with an affirmation or two that you can say to yourself.

_____

_____

_____

Continue Being Self-Compassionate

Embracing more positivity is an ongoing journey, and through that journey you need to remain compassionate toward yourself. Being self-critical is common. But you have learned that being kinder to yourself promotes more growth than being self-critical. Let's challenge any self-critical thoughts you have had recently and shift them toward self-compassion.

Self-Critical Thought	→	Self-Compassionate Thought
I'm not feeling happier. I'm failing at this.	→	_I'm working hard to feel more positive in my life._
_____	→	_____
_____	→	_____
_____	→	_____

Setting Limits or Boundaries

Knowing your limits is important to avoid overdoing things or experiencing increased levels of stress and exhaustion. Everyone has to-do lists to tend to and plays multiple roles in their day-to-day lives. How can you set your boundaries and allow yourself the time for daily self-care? Designating a time frame to complete a task and not going beyond that time frame can help you set limits, especially if you struggle with overdoing things. Fill in the weekly table to set some helpful limits or boundaries.

Time	8–10 a.m.	10 a.m.–12 p.m.	12–2 p.m.	2–4 p.m.	4–6 p.m.	6–8 p.m.
Mon					*End work*	
Tues	*Laundry*					
Wed						
Thurs						
Fri						*Self-care*
Sat		*Start cleaning*				
Sun		*Finish cleaning*	*Self-care*			

Check Out Your Thoughts!

As you explore automatic negative thoughts and ways to identify and cope with them, take them to the next step and examine the evidence. For instance, you may have the thought that you are not accomplishing enough at work, but by looking back at times when you have achieved tasks at work, you can successfully counter those automatic negative thoughts with concrete evidence.

Negative thought: *I'm not accomplishing my goals at work and will get fired.*

Check out the evidence: *I have always finished past projects even if I needed a little more time.*

Integrating a new thought: *Even if I miss a deadline, I'm still working hard toward my goals, and I haven't received any feedback that indicates I will get fired.*

Your negative thought: _____

Check out the evidence: _____

Integrating a new thought: _____

The Worry Train

Sometimes, when one worry appears, another worry will follow, like a worry train leaving the station to pick up the next worry. By taking account of each individual worry that elicits a subsequent one, you can begin to stop this worry train. Consider the following sequence of worries that get activated in your mind, and work on ways to interrupt the worries from taking off.

_____ → _____ → _____ →

I'm not cut out for this job.   *I'm terrible at all jobs.*   *I haven't made any friends at work.*

_____

I'm a failure at work and making friends.

Coping with Sadness or Loss

Sadness is a perfectly normal emotion to have, but it can be an uncomfortable one. When fostering a greater sense of happiness, the goal is not to rid yourself of sadness. Rather, the goal is to become more comfortable with weathering difficult feelings in a healthy, happiness-driven way and be more mindful and appreciative of positive moments and feelings. When sadness or loss occurs, notice the cadence of it and the way you experience it. During these times, exercise an increased amount of self-care and self-compassion. How do you positively cope with sadness and loss? Circle and consider ways you've coped.

Listen to music	Go for a walk	Journal	Connect with loved ones
Engage in a hobby	Exercise	Take a nap	Read a book
Meditate	Reflect with others who share a similar experience	Spend time outdoors	Other:

Where Do You Have Agency?

In some situations, you have agency, or control, over the situation, also known as an *internal locus of control*. In other situations, external factors determine the outcome, referred to as an *external locus of control*. Then there are times when you think you have control over a situation but you don't end up having control; this can lead to feelings of discomfort. If you can appropriately identify when you have agency in a situation, then you can feel rightfully motivated to make change. Consider situations in your life where you do have agency, where the control is internal and not due to external factors. During the times in which you have less agency, you can use your coping tools to process the situation.

Situations with External Locus of Control:
(e.g., work deadlines, reviews)

_____

Situations with Internal Locus of Control:
(e.g., productivity)

_____

During times in which you have less agency, or there is an external locus of control, consider the various tools in your coping toolbox that can reduce the intensity of your emotions.

Think in Probabilities, Not Possibilities

Anticipating events is common but can lead to worrisome thoughts. Thinking in probabilities, or the actual statistical chance a given event will occur, rather than possibilities, or believing an event may occur, can help you manage anxious thoughts or worries. For instance, if you receive an email from your boss saying she wants to meet to review your last project, you may begin to worry that you'll receive negative feedback. There is a possibility this could occur. But the probability that this will occur requires you to consider times in the past when this has occurred. If it hasn't occurred often in the past, then the probability of it happening is far less than any possibilities you can think of. Probabilities require an examination of evidence, while possibilities can include anything and may buy you a ticket on the worry train.

Anticipatory Event (e.g., results of a test)	Worrisome Thought (Possibility) (e.g., "I've failed")	Evidence to Support the Thought (Probability) Consider whether this event has happened to you before. How often or to what extent did the previous event occur? Does that fit the intensity of your worry? How did you overcome it? Were there moments of positivity that offset the negative feelings or experiences?

A Culmination of All Your Skills

Integrate the skills you have learned: assessing the situation, identifying negative thought patterns and feelings, folding in coping skills, and using the tools to transform a negative thought into a more positive and self-compassionate way of thinking. Once you're able to do this, congratulate yourself because you have attained the skills to address the harder times in order to foster happiness in your life. Use the following prompts to make an account of the most recent time you felt overwhelmed and stressed.

What was the situation? _____

What was the automatic negative thought? _____

What feelings did you experience? _____

What coping skill(s) did you use? *(breathing, distraction, checking out the evidence)*

_____

How can you transform your negative thought into a more self-compassionate thought?

_____

Dialectical Behavior Therapy

Dialectical behavior therapy (DBT) is a type of cognitive behavior therapy developed by Marsha M. Linehan in the 1970s. It focuses on changing negative thought patterns while shifting to more positive behaviors. The idea is to help individuals cope with uncomfortable emotions; it has been used to treat suicidal and self-harming behaviors. One premise of this approach is that uncomfortable feelings are transient, that feelings come and go. Using coping skills can help you focus on the fact that the discomfort will pass and that you can shift any maladaptive ways of coping to more positive methods. For example, the use of a distraction as a means to cope, such as refocusing your attention on cleaning until your emotions are more regulated and you feel calmer, is one of the techniques often used in DBT. Also used is "riding the wave," which means recognizing that a discomfort is transient and riding it out until an individual can process the situation in a more regulated and calm space. Often, DBT is practiced in a group-therapy format, but many of the interventions used can be applied in an individual setting as well.

Focus on Your Growth

When we set goals, we sometimes focus only on achievement of the desired outcome and fail to acknowledge what we did accomplish. By acknowledging progress toward (not just attainment of) the goal, you are rightfully granting yourself self-compassion and celebrating your accomplishments. Through this process, you can foster more growth toward your goals and gather more momentum and motivation to keep going. Map your growth in terms of how you have seen yourself move toward more happiness. Consider how you have been able to identify your negative thought patterns, engage in more positive thinking, and integrate more coping skills. Be specific with your achievements and celebrate your growth.

Areas Where I Have Grown	Areas Where I Wish to Continue to Grow
_____	_____
_____	_____
_____	_____
_____	_____

The more you are able to practice using these tools, the more readily you'll be able to address your negative thoughts, move through them, and spend more time happy. In addition to addressing the negative thoughts, by continuing routine self-care, both physical and mental, you will be able to continue working on your journey to bring more happiness into your life.

> I have grown in my ability to notice my feelings, challenge some of my thoughts, and shift some of my actions in order to integrate new skills and be a better, happier person. I have done the heavy lifting work, and I'm continuing to map out my personal journey for my continued growth.

CONCLUSION

This chapter will help you maintain your new skills for the long-term by reevaluating your routines, refining the tools you have used, and integrating all of the techniques into your life in order to embrace ways to combat negativity and embrace more positivity. Sustaining change can be a challenge because change is not linear. Keep in mind that there may be obstacles on your journey to happiness. Emotional states such as sadness, anger, disappointment, or loss will still be part of the human experience. Be patient with yourself. Be self-compassionate. Be mindful of your emotions and aware that though these times arise, we are prepared to experience them and move through them when necessary. And return to this workbook when you need to remind yourself of a skill. Making the personal commitment to continue to seek more enjoyment in life and engaging in the hard work to do it will pay off in growth and change.

"You may not control all
the events that happen
to you, but you can decide
not to be reduced by them."

—MAYA ANGELOU

EMBRACING A HAPPIER LIFE

Congratulations on completing the *Happiness Workbook*. I am so proud of all of the hard work you've done. You have engaged in very challenging skills, such as recognizing thought patterns, challenging your thinking, and embracing more cognitive flexibility. You were open to trying new coping skills, such as being more present, engaging your physical self, shifting your environment, and improving the quality of your connections. Take the time to acknowledge yourself for your accomplishments!

While you may be at the end of the workbook, you are in many wonderful ways at the beginning of your happiness journey. This is your opportunity to reflect on and incorporate the various exercises and practices that felt natural for you to do and that folded easily into your life. Continued practice of the skills that were more difficult for you will help you build your muscles in these abilities, and eventually these will fold into your life as well.

Occasionally, you may find yourself needing reminders on how to use certain tools, or you may want to integrate techniques you practiced in this workbook that you didn't initially add to your repertoire. You can always revisit sections of this workbook to build on skills like mindfulness or healing your body. You now possess a variety of tools and know which tools work the best for you in certain situations. By continuing to use the tools, you will find that they become more automatic in nature. You will start to build and solidify a neural pathway to which you will eventually default when coping.

Take note of where you are in this journey and the direction you wish to continue to go, and remember that happiness is not a destination but an ongoing journey that takes continued work, practice, and evolution. Continuing to evaluate where you are in the journey can help you remain on track toward your goals.

RESOURCES

For additional support should symptoms of sadness and worry persist, please call the National Suicide Prevention Hotline at 1-800-273-TALK (8255) or text HOME to 741-741 for 24-7 crisis support.

The Substance Abuse and Mental Health Services Administration (SAMHSA) National Helpline for free, confidential support 24-7, 365 days a year for people facing mental health challenges can be reached at 1-800-662-HELP (4357).

For more information on anxiety disorders and to begin to get the help you may need, please visit NIMH.NIH.gov/health/topics/anxiety-disorders/index.shtml.

For more information on depression and to begin to get the help you may need, please visit NIMH.NIH.gov/health/topics/depression/index.shtml.

Should you seek a therapist in your area but struggle to locate one, use a listserv such as the one available on PsychologyToday.com.

REFERENCES

Angelou, Maya. 2008. *Letter to My Daughter*. New York: Random House.

Bailey, Thomas C., Winnie Eng, Michael B. Frisch, and C. R. Snyder. 2007. "Hope and Optimism as Related to Life Satisfaction." *Journal of Positive Psychology* 2, no. 3: 168–169.

Barton, Jo and Mike Rogerson. 2017. "The Importance of Greenspace for Mental Health." *BJPsych International* 14, no. 4 (January 2): 79–81. doi.org/10.1192/s2056474000002051.

Bastiaansen, Jojanneke, Marc Thioux, and Christian Keysers. 2009. "Evidence for Mirror Systems in Emotions." *Philosophical Transactions of the Royal Society of London*, Series B, Biological Sciences 364, no. 1528 (August 27): 2391–2404. doi.org/10.1098/rstb.2009.0058.

Bausum, Ann. 2007. *Our Country's First Ladies*. Washington, DC: National Geographic Kids.

Beck, Judith S. 1995. *Cognitive Therapy: Basics and Beyond*. New York: The Guilford Press.

Bellet, Clement, Jan-Emmanuel De Neve, and George Ward. 2019. "Does Employee Happiness Have an Impact on Productivity?" *Saïd Business School WP 2019-13* (October 14). dx.doi.org/10.2139/ssrn.3470734.

Bremner, J. Douglas. 2006. "Traumatic Stress: Effects on the Brain." *Dialogues in Clinical Neuroscience* 8, no. 4: 445–461. doi.org/10.31887/DCNS.2006.8.4/jbremner.

Brosschot, Jos F., Bart Verkuil, and Julian F. Thayer. 2016. "The Default Response to Uncertainty and the Importance of Perceived Safety in Anxiety and Stress: An Evolution-Theoretical Perspective." *Journal of Anxiety Disorders* 41 (June): 22–34.

Brown, Joshua, and Joel Wong. 2017. "How Gratitude Changes You and Your Brain." *Greater Good Magazine*, Greater Good Science Center at the University of California, Berkeley (June 6). GreaterGood.Berkeley.edu/article/item/how_gratitude_changes_you_and_your_brain.

Bruine de Bruin, Wändi, Andrew M. Parker, and JoNell Strough. 2020. "Age Differences in Reported Social Networks and Well-Being." *Psychology and Aging* 35, no. 2 (March): 159–168. doi.org/10.1037/pag0000415.

Catalino, Lahnna. 2015. "A Better Way to Pursue Happiness." *Greater Good Magazine*, Greater Good Science Center at the University of California, Berkeley (July 13). GreaterGood.Berkeley.edu/article/item/a_better_way_to_pursue_happiness.

Catalino, Lahnna I., Sara B. Algoe, Barbara L. Fredrickson. 2014. "Prioritizing Positivity: An Effective Approach to Pursuing Happiness?" *Emotion* 14, no. 6 (December): 1155–1161. doi.org/10.1037/a0038029.

Chapman, Alexander L. 2006. "Dialectical Behavior Therapy: Current Indications and Unique Elements." *Psychiatry* 3, no. 9 (September): 62–68.

Cheng, Helen, and Adrian Furnham. 2002. "Personality, Peer Relationships, and Self-Confidence as Predictors of Happiness and Loneliness." *Journal of Adolescence* 25, no. 3 (June): 327–339. doi.org/10.1006/jado.2002.0475.

Cohen, Geoffrey L. and David K. Sherman. 2014. "The Psychology of Change: Self-Affirmation and Social Psychological Interventions." *Annual Review of Psychology* 65: 333–371. doi.org/10.1146/annurev-psych-010213-115137.

Cohut, Maria. 2018. "What Are the Health Benefits of Being Social?" *Medical News Today* (February 23). MedicalNewsToday.com/articles/321019.

Connors, Charlotte. 2008. *How Dolly Parton Saved My Life: A Novel of the Jelly Jar Sisterhood*. New York: Broadway Books.

Costanzo, Erin S., Susan K. Lutgendorf, Marian L. Kohut, Nicole Nisly, Kayla Rozeboom, Shawn Spooner, JoAnn Benda, and Janet E. McElhaney. 2004. "Mood and Cytokine Response to Influenza Virus in Older Adults." *The Journals of Gerontology* Series A59, no. 12 (December): 1328–1333. doi.org/10.1093/gerona/59.12.1328.

Deslandes, Andréa, Helena Moraes, Camila Ferreira, Heloisa Veiga, Heitor Silveira, Raphael Mouta, Fernando A. M. S. Pompeu, Evandro Silva Freire Coutinho, and Jerson Laks. 2009. "Exercise and Mental Health: Many Reasons to Move." *Neuropsychobiology* 59, no. 4: 191–198.

Dfarhud, Dariush, Maryam Malmir, and Mohammad Khanahmadi. 2014. "Happiness & Health: The Biological Factors-Systematic Review Article." *Iranian Journal of Public Health* 43, no. 11 (November): 1468–1477.

Diener, Ed and Robert A. Emmons. 1984. "The Independence of Positive and Negative Affect." *Journal of Personality and Social Psychology* 47, no. 5 (November): 1105–1117. doi.org/10.1037/0022-3514.47.5.1105.

Diener, Ed, Eunkook M. Suh, Richard E. Lucas, and Heidi L. Smith. 1999. "Subjective Well-Being: Three Decades of Progress." *Psychological Bulletin* 125, no. 2 (March): 276–302. doi.org/10.1037/0033-2909.125.2.276.

Driessen, Ellen and Steven D. Hollon. 2010. "Cognitive Behavioral Therapy for Mood Disorders: Efficacy, Moderators and Mediators." *The Psychiatric Clinics of North America* 33, no. 3 (September): 537–555. doi.org/10.1016/j.psc.2010.04.005.

Dyer, Wayne W. 2001. *There's a Spiritual Solution to Every Problem*. New York: HarperCollins.

Firth, Joseph, James E. Gangwisch, Alessandra Borsini, Robyn E. Wootton, and Emeran A. Mayer. 2020. "Food and Mood: How Do Diet and Nutrition Affect Mental Wellbeing?" *The British Medical Journal* 369 (June 29). doi.org/10.1136/bmj.m2382.

Gerrig, Richard J. and Philip G. Zimbardo. 2009. *Psychology and Life* (19th ed.). New York: Pearson.

Grossman, Paul, Ludwig Kappos, Henrik Gensicke, Marcus D'Souza, David C. Mohr, Ik Penner, and Claudia Steiner. 2010. "MS Quality of Life, Depression, and Fatigue Improve after Mindfulness Training: A Randomized Trial." *Neurology* 75, no. 13 (September 28): 1141–1149. doi.org/10.1212/WNL.0b013e3181f4d80d.

Heydari, Mostafa, Saideh Masafi, Mehdi Jafari, Seyed Hassan Saadat, and Shima Shahyad. 2018. "Effectiveness of Acceptance and Commitment Therapy on Anxiety and Depression of Razi Psychiatric Center Staff." *Open Access Macedonian Journal of Medical Sciences* 6, no. 2 (February 15): 410–415. doi.org/10.3889/oamjms.2018.064.

Hills, Peter and Michael Argyle. 2002. "The Oxford Happiness Questionnaire: A Compact Scale for the Measurement of Psychological Well-Being." *Personality and Individual Differences* 33, no. 7 (November): 1073–1082. doi.org/10.1016/S0191-8869(01)00213-6.

Hofmann, Stefan G., Alice T. Sawyer, Ashley A. Witt, and Diana Oh. 2010. "The Effect of Mindfulness-Based Therapy on Anxiety and Depression: A Meta-Analytic Review." *Journal of Consulting and Clinical Psychology* 78, no. 2 (April): 169–183.

Hofmann, Stefan G., Anu Asnaani, Imke J. J. Vonk, Alice T. Sawyer, and Angela Fang. 2012. "The Efficacy of Cognitive Behavioral Therapy: A Review of Meta-Analyses." *Cognitive Therapy and Research* 36, no. 5 (July 31): 427–440. doi.org/10.1007/s10608-012-9476-1.

Houston, Elaine. 2020. "19 Positive Psychology Exercises to Do with Clients or Students." PositivePsychology.com. Accessed September 1, 2020. PositivePsychology.com/positive-psychology-exercises.

Jennings, Lea B. 1997. "Potential Benefits of Pet Ownership in Health Promotion." *Journal of Holistic Nursing* 15, no. 4 (December): 358–372. doi.org/10.1177/089801019701500404.

Jung, C. G. and Sonu Shamdasani (editor). 2012. *The Red Book: A Reader's Edition*. New York: W. W. Norton.

Kilner, James M., and Roger N. Lemon. 2013. "What We Know Currently about Mirror Neurons." *Current Biology* 23, no. 23 (December 2): PR1057–R1062. doi.org/10.1016/j.cub.2013.10.051.

Kim, Eui-Joong, and Joel E. Dimsdale. 2007. "The Effect of Psychosocial Stress on Sleep: A Review of Polysomnographic Evidence." *Behavioral Sleep Medicine* 5, no. 4 (December 5): 256–278. doi.org/10.1080/15402000701557383.

Kolacz, Jacek, Katja K. Kovacic, and Stephen W. Porges. 2019. "Traumatic Stress and the Autonomic Brain-Gut Connection in Development: Polyvagal Theory as an Integrative Framework for Psychosocial and Gastrointestinal Pathology." *Developmental Psychobiology* 61, no. 5 (April 5). doi.org/10.1002/dev.21852.

Koo, Minkyung, Sara B. Algoe, Timothy D. Wilson, and Daniel T. Gilbert. 2008. "It's a Wonderful Life: Mentally Subtracting Positive Events Improves People's Affective States, Contrary to Their Affective Forecasts." *Journal of Personality and Social Psychology* 95, no. 5 (November): 1217–1224. doi.org/10.1037/a0013316.

Kop, Willem J., Stephen J. Synowski, Miranda E. Newell, Louis A. Schmidt, Shari R. Waldstein, and Nathan A. Fox. 2011. "Autonomic Nervous System Reactivity to Positive and Negative Mood Induction: The Role of Acute Psychological Responses and Frontal Electrocortical Activity." *Biological Psychology* 86, no. 3 (March): 230–238. doi.org/10.1016/j.biopsycho.2010.12.003.

Lambert, Craig. 2007. "The Science of Happiness: Psychology Explores Humans at Their Best." *Harvard Magazine*, January-February 2007. HarvardMagazine.com /2007/01/the-science-of-happiness.html.

Lewis, C. S. 1960. *The Four Loves*. New York: Harcourt Brace.

Lorde, Audre. 2004. *Conversations with Audre Lorde*. Jackson, MS: University Press of Mississippi.

Miller, Kelly. 2020. "CBT Explained: An Overview and Summary of CBT." PositivePsychology.com (January 9). PositivePsychology.com/cbt.

Muha, Tom. 2016. "Achieving Happiness: Using Cognitive Behavioral Therapy to Combat Anxiety." CapitalGazette.com (October 16). CapitalGazette.com /lifestyles/ph-ac-muha-1016-20161016-story.html.

Ohrnberger, Julius, Eleonora Fichera, and Matt Sutton. 2017. "The Relationship between Physical and Mental Health: A Mediation Analysis." *Social Science & Medicine* 195 (December): 42–49.

O'Neil, Adrienne, Shae E. Quirk, Siobhan Housden, Sharon L. Brennan, Lana J. Williams, Julie A. Pasco, Michael Berk, and Felice N. Jacka. 2014. "Relationship between Diet and Mental Health in Children and Adolescents: A Systematic Review." *American Journal of Public Health* 104, no. 10 (October): e31–e42. doi.org/10.2105/AJPH.2014.302110.

Pietrangelo, Ann. 2019. "9 CBT Techniques for Better Mental Health." Healthline.com (December 12). Healthline.com/health/cbt-techniques.

Prochaska, James O. and Carlo C. DiClemente. 1983. "Stages and Processes of Self-Change of Smoking: Toward an Integrative Model of Change." *Journal of Consulting and Clinical Psychology* 51, no. 3 (June): 390–395. doi.org /10.1037/0022-006X.51.3.390.

Purves, Dale, George J. Augustine, David Fitzpatrick, Lawrence C. Katz, Anthony -Samuel LaMantia, James O. McNamara, and S. Mark Williams, editors. 2001. "Physiological Changes Associated with Emotion." *Neuroscience* (2nd ed.). Sunderland, MA: Sinauer Associates.

Ritchie, Deanna. 2018. "9 Ways Being a Happier Person Increases Productivity." Calendar.com (November 22). Calendar.com/blog/9-ways-being-a-happier -person-increases-productivity.

Rizzo, Flavio. 2016. "Hikikomori: The Postmodern Hermits of Japan." Warscapes.com (June 14). Warscapes.com/opinion/hikikomori-postmodern-hermits-japan.

Rohrer, Julia M., David Richter, Martin Brümmer, Gert G. Wagner, and Stefan C. Schmukle. 2018. "Successfully Striving for Happiness: Socially Engaged Pursuits Predict Increases in Life Satisfaction." *Psychological Science* 29, no. 8 (August): 1291–1298.

Rumi, Maryam Mafi, and Azima Melita Kolin. 2012. *Rumi's Little Book of Life: The Garden of the Soul, the Heart, and the Spirit*. Charlottesville, VA: Hampton Roads Publishing Company.

Russo-Netzer, Pninit. 2019. "Why You Should Prioritize Meaning in Your Everyday Life." *Greater Good Magazine* (March 6). GreaterGood.Berkeley.edu/article/item /why_you_should_prioritize_meaning_in_your_everyday_life.

Sapranaviciute-Zabazlajeva, Laura, Dalia Luksiene, Dalia Virviciute, Martin Bobak, and Abdonas Tamosiunas. 2017. "Link between Healthy Lifestyle and Psycholog-ical Well-Being in Lithuanian Adults Aged 45–72: A Cross-Sectional Study." *The British Medical Journal Open* 7, no. 4 (April 3). NCBI.NLM.NIH.gov/pmc/articles /PMC5387968.

Schneider, David, Albert Hastorf, and Phoebe Ellsworth. 1979. *Person Perception* (2nd ed.). Reading, MA: Addison-Wesley.

Seligman, Martin E. P. 2002. *Authentic Happiness: Using the New Positive Psychology to Realize Your Potential for Lasting Fulfillment*. New York: Simon & Schuster.

Seligman, Martin. 2018. "PERMA and the Building Blocks of Well-Being." *Journal of Positive Psychology* 13, no. 4 (February 16): 333–335. doi.org/10.1080/17439760 .2018.1437466.

Shultz, Susanne, Christopher Opie, and Quentin D. Atkinson. 2011. "Stepwise Evolution of Stable Sociality in Primates." *Nature* 479 (November 9): 219–222. doi.org/10.1038/nature10601.

Slepian, Michael L., Simon N. Ferber, Joshua M. Gold, and Abraham M. Rutchick. 2015. "The Cognitive Consequences of Formal Clothing." *Social Psychological and Personality Science* 6, no. 6 (March 31): 661–668. doi.org/10.1177 /1948550615579462.

Smyth, Joshua, Margit C. Ockenfels, Laura Porter, Clemens Kirschbaum, Dirk H. Hellhammer, and Arthur A. Stone. 1998. "Stressors and Mood Measured on a Momentary Basis Are Associated with Salivary Cortisol Secretion." *Psychoneuroendocrinology* 23, no. 4 (May): 353–370. doi.org/10.1016 /S0306-4530(98)00008-0.

Star, Katharina. 2020. "How to Overcome All-or-Nothing Thinking." VeryWellMind .com (May 25). VeryWellMind.com/all-or-nothing-thinking-2584173.

Steimer, Thierry. 2002. "The Biology of Fear– and Anxiety–Related Behaviors." *Dialogues in Clinical Neuroscience* 4, no. 3 (September): 231–249. doi.org /10.31887/DCNS.2002.4.3/tsteimer.

Steptoe, Andrew, E. Leigh Gibson, Mark Hamer, and Jane Wardle. 2007. "Neuroendo-crine and Cardiovascular Correlates of Positive Affect Measured by Ecological Momentary Assessment and by Questionnaire." *Psychoneuroendocrinology* 32, no. 1 (January): 56–64. doi.org/10.1016/j.psyneuen.2006.10.001.

Steptoe, Andrew, Katie O'Donnell, Michael Marmot, and Jane Wardle. 2008. "Positive Affect, Psychological Well-Being, and Good Sleep." *Journal of Psychosomatic Research* 64, no. 4 (April): 409–415. doi.org/10.1016/j.jpsychores.2007.11.008.

Strand, Elin B., Alex J. Zautra, Magne Thoresen, Sigrid Ødegård, Till Uhlig, and Arnstein Finset. 2006. "Positive Affect as a Factor of Resilience in the Pain–Negative Affect Relationship in Patients with Rheumatoid Arthritis." *Journal of Psychosomatic Research* 60, no. 5 (May): 477–484. doi.org/10.1016/j.jpsychores.2005.08.010.

Tooby, John and Leda Cosmides. 2008. "The Evolutionary Psychology of the Emotions and Their Relationship to Internal Regulatory Variables." In *Handbook of Emotions*, edited by Lisa Feldman Barrett, Michael Lewis, and Jeanette M. Haviland-Jones, 114–137. New York: The Guilford Press.

Umberson, Debra, and Jennifer Karas Montez. 2010. "Social Relationships and Health: A Flashpoint for Health Policy." *Journal of Health and Social Behavior* 51 (Supplement): S54–S66. doi.org/10.1177/0022146510383501.

von Furstenberg, Diane. 1998. *Diane: A Signature Life*. New York: Simon & Schuster.

Waxenbaum, Joshua A., Vamsi Reddy, and Matthew Varacallo. 2020. "Anatomy, Autonomic Nervous System." StatPearls Publishing. Last modified August 10, 2020. NCBI.NLM.NIH.gov/books/NBK539845.

Zhang, Chun-Qing, Emily Leeming, Patrick Smith, Pak-Kwong Chung, Martin S. Hagger, and Steven C. Hayes. 2018. "Acceptance and Commitment Therapy for Health Behavior Change: A Contextually-Driven Approach." *Frontiers in Psychology* 8 (January 11). doi.org/10.3389/fpsyg.2017.02350.

INDEX

ACKNOWLEDGMENTS

I'd like to acknowledge my husband, who spared the extra hours in order for me to complete this book. I am also grateful to my parents, who are my forever supporters throughout my journey.

Finally, a special thanks to my children, who inspire me to embrace the many joys in life.

ABOUT THE AUTHOR

 Anna Napawan, PhD, is a licensed clinical psychologist practicing in California, where she resides with her family in the Bay Area. She earned her PhD in Clinical Psychology from Palo Alto University. Dr. Napawan has worked and trained in a variety of settings, including UCSF Langley Porter Psychiatric Hospital and Clinic, Children's Hospital Oakland, The Wright Institute, Ann Martin Center, and Kaiser Permanente. She currently works in private practice with children, families, and adults in assessing and treating anxiety, depression, trauma, ADHD, and ASD. Her approach is holistic, using empirical and efficacious interventions with socially just and systemic views while folding evolutionary concepts into her work.